01627945

D1580065

ALONG
A HIGHLAND
ROAD

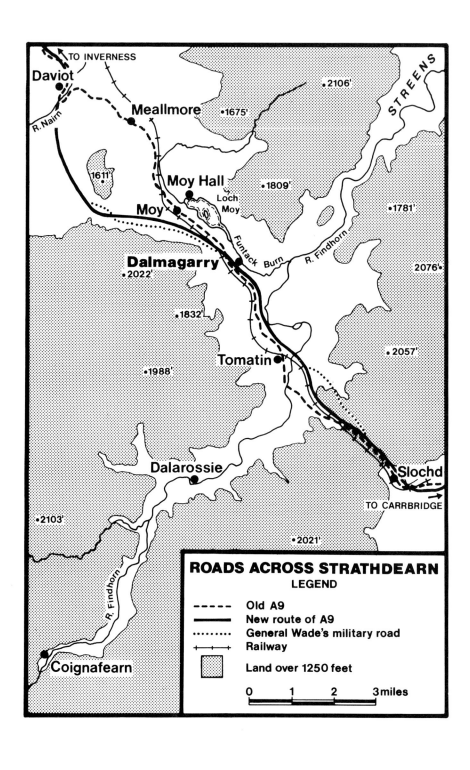

ROADS ACROSS STRATHDEARN

LEGEND

- – – – Old A9
- ——— New route of A9
- ·········· General Wade's military road
- +–+–+ Railway
- ▦ Land over 1250 feet

0 1 2 3 miles

ALONG
A HIGHLAND
ROAD

I.F. GRANT MBE LLD

With thirty-one illustrations
and three maps

Shepheard-Walwyn

First published in 1980 by
Shepheard-Walwyn (Publishers) Limited
51 Vineyard Hill Road, London SW19 7JL

ISBN 0 85683 048 8

Typeset by
Specialised Offset Services Limited, Liverpool
Printed in Great Britain by
Whitstable Litho Limited, Kent

For Catherine Dickson
To whom I owe the happiness
of writing this book

Acknowledgements

This book has been written in happy co-operation with my brother, Eneas, my nephew, Patrick, my friends and colleagues, Catherine Dickson, Murdo MacAskill and George Dixon. Without their help, I could not have done it and to them is due my warmest thanks. I also keep in grateful remembrance all that I learnt in the past from Duncan Davidson, Jimmie Dunbar and Annie Noble. I am very grateful to Michael Matthews for allowing me to read his aunt, Lady Malkin's, memoirs, to P.A. Anderson for his helpful maps, to Rosalind Marshall, James Holloway, Hugh Gray Cheape, G. Howat, Eric Cregeen, Mary Mackintosh, Anna Calder, Nial Macpherson, Margaret Gerrard, Catriona McClements, Jacqueline Milligan and the staff of Edinburgh Public Library for help in many ways.

For permission to publish copyright illustrations my thanks to Mackintosh of Mackintosh, the Commissioner for the Preservation of the Ancient Monuments of Scotland, the National Galleries of Scotland, the Scottish National Portrait Gallery, the Highland Folk Museum (Kingussie), the *Scots Magazine*, the Highland Wild Life Park (Aviemore), Inverness District Council, the National Museum of Antiquities of Scotland, Messrs Johnston and Bacon and the British Library. For permission to quote from *Scottish Verse from the Book of the Dean of Lismore* edited by W.J. Watson my thanks to Scottish Academic Press.

In this peaceful place I have been enabled to set down the fugitive recollections of old age.

I.F. GRANT

Viewpoint Guest House
Edinburgh

1980

Contents

List of Illustrations and Maps

1

The Road

It is fine to bowl along the new stretches of the A9 unhampered by slowly moving traffic, unharassed by blind corners. If one was familiar with the old road one has memories to spare of vexatious delays and awkward moments. Nevertheless, one has other associations, for ancient tales and traditions tend to cling to old roads and, if one can identify a definite place, it gives the vaguest of stories a touch of reality. For this reason I have written down what I can remember about the dozen or so miles of the old A9 where it crosses Strathdearn. Some are remembrances of the very different every-day life of my own family when I was young or what I was told, when my parents and grandparents were in a reminiscing mood, about manners and customs in Victorian and Edwardian times. Some are old tales that I grew up with or that I owe to the generosity of friendly neighbours who recalled for my benefit their own family traditions. My kinsmen who work and live in Strathdearn have helped me over practical details. I myself have had many years of browsing in Highland history and anything that concerned Strathdearn stuck in my memory. All these bits and pieces I have tried to string together on a strand of historical continuity (and all too often only of probability!). In making a folk museum one is limited to concrete things, in writing Highland history to facts for which there is documentary evidence. This book is only limited by the meanderings of the old road.

The place now known as the Slock is the best place to start from in following the dozen or so miles of road that cross Strathdearn. Slochd Muic, to give it its old name, was an obvious way to take from Strath Spey to Strathdearn and Captain Burt, writing about 1736, gives rather a horrific account of the old track that ran down it. The name means Hole of the Pig or, more romantically, Lair of the Wild Boar. The wild boar was a formidable woodlander. His grim visage is proudly emblazoned on the coats of arms of a number of Scots families. He flourished when the Caledonian Forest of pine trees still covered much of Strath Spey and when Strathdearn was largely forested with birch and hazel. They are still the natural trees of the district and the moss hags are full of their remains. Although pine and fir are the trees mainly planted because they are commercially valuable, they do not flourish as in Strath Spey. In these inland straths people seldom used cruisie lamps, instead they used splinters of resinous pine wood to give them light in the winter. Sir Aeneas Mackintosh in his *Notes* (written about the 1770s) recalls how the people used to toast these 'fir candles' and set them in a circle on a stone; the youngest person present had to tend them.[1] And I have been told that people used to make a special expedition every autumn to Strath Spey to gather a supply of resinous wood – the very best for the purpose were the stumps of tree roots buried in the moss.

Old people have told me that 'Once upon a time there were only three smokes (i.e. human habitations) in Strathdearn', and the word Free = *Frithe* = Forest, appears in several place names including that of the Freeburn Hotel. The Forest of Strathdearn is mentioned in official documents of the twelfth century.

Wolves, like wild boars, were forest dwellers and the last wolf to be killed in the district (and claimed to be the last wolf killed in Scotland) was slain in 1743 close to the entrance to the Streens – the narrow defile through which the Findhorn finds its way to the sea. Mackintosh of Mackintosh had trysted a party to hunt the beast down and MacQueen of Pollochaig was late in joining them. When he appeared Mackintosh reproached him for his lateness and MacQueen produced the wolf's head. He had met and killed the beast with his dirk.

The Highlanders peopled their country with more formidable beings than the wild boars or the wolves. There are several variants of a tale about a kelpie that lived in a deep pool at the bottom of Slochd Muic. It has been obliterated by the road and railway embankments, but there used to be a sombre-looking pond close to the road bridge over the railway where a sinister being like a kelpie might like to dabble its feet. Kelpies are common in Highland folklore. They lived in pools or rivers or lochs and, taking the form of a beautiful horse, would try to cajole an unwary passerby to mount. The passerby's hand would stick to the kelpie when he touched it and the kelpie would then dash into the water and devour him.

One evening a man named Willox was returning through the Slochd from a convivial meeting and the kelpie accosted him. Being, as the saying is, 'not drunk but happy in himself', Willox grabbed the kelpie's bridle close to the bit and this gave him complete power over it. Eventually the kelpie managed to escape, but it did not return to its evil ways at the pool.

There are two interesting points about this tale. It seems probable that many kelpie stories originate from some special hazard in the piece of water that they are said to inhabit. In the case of a Strath Nairn kelpie, the lochan that he inhabited was on the estate of Brin, which at one time belonged to a family of Stuarts with whom I sometimes stayed and who told me that when a water spaniel got into difficulties while retrieving a duck, it was discovered that the lochan was infested with a kind of water-weed difficult to swim through. In the case of Slochd Muic, Burt wrote that a stream from the pool sometimes overflowed onto the steep paths leading from the Slochd, and that the rushing water was far more dangerous if one were going downhill than if one were breasting the slope and the current.

The name Willox, the hero of the tale, is an unexpected one to find in a Highland strath, but I had come across it in an eighteenth-century rental dealing with the upper part of the Strath. Mr George Dixon, whose knowledge of Strath Spey is encyclopaedic, gave me details of the family tree. They were, in fact, MacGregors who took the name Willocks or Willox when their own was proscribed; like many other members of their clan, they found asylum in Strath Spey. It is a matter of pride to me that one of my Grant forebears was among the Grants who were fined by the Scots Privy Council for giving succour to MacGregors. A member of the Willox family, named John, is on record as living in Easter Raigmore Farm between 1718 and 1735 and is evidently the hero of the tale. His grandson became factor of the Grant estates in Strath Spey and his great-grandson, who resumed the name MacGregor, was a distinguished doctor in London, appointed physician to George IV, and made a baronet. His illegitimate grandson, however, followed the unusual career of 'cow doctor' and wizard. He worked his cures with water into which a magic pebble or a bit of an old horse's bit had been dipped. He was known as Willox the Warlock and died in 1833 as duly recorded in an obituary notice in the *Inverness Courier* of the time.

One wonders if Willox's name was attached to an existing kelpie story belonging to the Slochd or if it was imported to fit him. In either case it illustrates the tendency, which crops up again and again, to connect the occult with incomers or prehistoric remains.

Remote and wild as it undoubtedly was, Strathdearn Forest was not virgin. In preparing the archaeological section of the Ordnance Survey, traces were found of scattered groups of small hut circles and also of an ancient form of cultivation on the rising ground on each side of the river near the present village of Tomatin. Hut circles of a similar type were found near Nairn and they have been dated as far back as the third millennium BC. One wonders if an expanding society led the people who made these circles to penetrate inland so far as Strathdearn or if, and more probably, the Strathdearn settlement was the last refuge of a fugitive race. All memory or tradition of these people has disappeared but traces of their occupation probably contributed to the fairy-lore of later times.[2]

A description survives of what the Slochd was like before it was filled by a succession of four roads and the railway. Captain Burt, who came to the North about 1725, on work for the government, and who wrote the well-known series of *Letters from a Gentleman in the North of Scotland*, described the Slochd in a letter about a journey from Inverness to Strath Spey. He thought it advisable to hire a guide. He gave a dramatic account of crossing the boggy ground near Moy and when he came to the Slochd he 'found it most horrible'. He described the mountains on either side as precipitous. There was a lake at the bottom, the path was only two feet wide and the slope so steep that, as he rode, the water seemed to be under his stirrup and he estimated that the drop was twice as high as the Cross of St Paul's from Ludgate Hill.[3]

Burt was not unduly prejudiced. Even after General Wade had made his road, the Slochd appeared as a grim place to more sympathetic travellers. Bishop Forbes (to whom we owe that priceless collection of first-hand recollections of the '45, *The Lyon in Mourning*) wrote in his 1762 Journal that in the Slochd you could see nothing but the Heavens above and a hill on either side, 'that on ye Right being one of the most bleak, rugged, scraggy Objects ever seen; and yet upon it there is plenty of large, juicy wild Strawberries of a Flavour peculiarly fine'.[4]

The first road was made by General Wade as part of a comprehensive plan for the pacification of the Highlands. As the feudal due of military service fell into disuse all over the rest of Britain, the continued internal warfare among the clans made the Highlands more and more politically important. This possible menace was much increased after the

Field Marshal George Wade: in the background making of road over Corriearrack. Attributed to J. van Diest, Scottish National Portrait Gallery.

Hanoverian succession had brought about the Jacobite movement. Unlucky and ill-organized as the Rising of the '15 had been, it had illustrated the mettle of the clans who supported the cause of the Stuarts.

General Wade was appointed Commander-in-Chief for Scotland in 1724 and he proceeded to carry out a four-point plan:

To raise Independent Companies of Highlanders from the clans well affected to the government, dressed and armed and well versed in local ways, to keep law and order.

To carry out a general policy of disarmament.

To establish permanent military posts at places of strategic importance.

To construct roads that would give the military rapid access to these posts.

In 1728 he began the road from Dunkeld to Inverness, where there was a military garrison.[5] It took him two years and, with his admirable eye for the lie of the land, of all the various routes over the hills used by the Highlanders he chose to build the road over Drumochter and through the Slochd. He thus standardized the way north that those bound to wheel transport have taken ever since.

Making the road was a military exercise, carried out by companies of 100 men with officers, non-commissioned officers and a drummer, and rest camps were established every ten miles. It was anticipated that the roads might have to be made through unfriendly country. So it is recorded by Sir Aeneas Mackintosh that Wade, before he planned the section that crossed Strathdearn, wrote to Lachlan Mackintosh of Mackintosh 'desiring to know in what direction he wished to have the road carried through his estate, and that he would desire his people not to molest his workmen'.[6]

Clan Mackintosh had taken a distinguished part in the '15 and the Chief and some of his leading men (including my great-great-great-grandfather) had been imprisoned for a short time. He had, however, made his peace with the government and so no untoward incident occurred while the road was made through Strathdearn. One of the rest camps was made at Dalmagarry, halfway across the valley.

Wade's roads were made for military purposes and not for civilian traffic. The passage through the Slochd was particularly difficult. Sir Aeneas himself wrote, 'The descent into the hollow is so sudden, and the turn round the hill so unexpected that if your horses are not very peaceable, you would better alight and have them led thro' it.'[7] Another

Survey Party at Kinloch Rannoch employed upon official survey of the Highlands, 1745-53. By Paul Sanby, National Gallery of Scotland.

defect as many travellers and Sir Aeneas himself complained, was that the deep, narrow cleft was liable to be snowed up – occasionally for weeks at a time.

A more serious danger was that the Slochd became a haunt for thieves. A minor tragedy was described by 'The Highland Lady' (Miss Elizabeth Grant of Rothiemurchus). In 1808 her aunt was on her way to her marriage in Inverness and the little trunk, containing the trousseau she had been sewing all through the summer and which had been tied on 'under the rumble', was found to have been cut off by some rascally Highlander 'in the dreary waste named from the wild boors'.[8]

There were, however, grimmer robberies. About the middle of the eighteenth century the Slochd became the haunt of a gang led by Edward Mackintosh of Borlum, grandson of 'The Brigadier' (whose story comes later in my memories of the road) and of kin to that very distinguished citizen of Inverness Aeneas Mackintosh MP. Anderson's admirable *Guide* described Edward as 'a man of education and respectable family and of insinuating manners. He had a good deal of the old mercenary soldier about him, with an air of French politeness which was common in the Highland gentleman of the period; and though secretly leagued with a gang of desperadoes, he continued for a long time to deceive the public and lull the suspicions of his friends'.[9] There were many general allegations about the misdeeds of the gang and it was said that they used to dig graves for their expected victims. The member of the gang who turned King's Evidence alluded to several murders but in their trial, which took place in 1773, only two crimes were alleged: that of robbing the house of the weaver of Killiehuntly (in Strath Spey) and that in which they were caught, an attempt to rob Sir Hector Monro of Novar on his return from service in India. Three of Borlum's accomplices, one of whom was his illegitimate brother, were caught and two were tried and hanged in Inverness, the third having turned King's Evidence and was pardoned.[10] The others fled the country and Borlum is said to have served under General Washington and, finally, to have returned to Scotland.

The planning of the new road that is at present being constructed by the most modern scientific and technological methods, is a tribute to the innate genius of General Wade, for it frequently takes the same line as did his military road built about 250 years ago. Unfortunately, a great deal of the remains of his road that one used to be able to trace have been obliterated. From the Slochd it could be plainly seen, running almost parallel to the later road but veering eastwards to a ford across the Findhorn almost below the railway viaduct. It then ran through the low ground along the river, but at a point where the river turns eastwards it took advantage of a gentle slope and rose to higher ground. The roads, old and new, and the railway cross each other and traces of Wade's road are lost. But about Moy it follows a different and more westerly line across the open moorland – the Plain = *Magh* from which Moy gets its name. In doing so it was following a much older track that descended to the Nairn by a glen known as the Threshold of the Highlands = Stairsneach nan Gaidheal. It crossed the Nairn near the present Faillie Bridge and from that point on to Inverness it has been covered by a road still in use and which, as it approaches Inverness, is known as The Old Edinburgh Road, a name that thrilled me as a child.

While still under military administration, a second layer in the conglomeration of roads at the Slochd was carried through by General Wade's Inspector of Roads, Major William Caulfeild, generally known in his own day as Governor Caulfeild because he was Deputy Governor of Inverness Castle. He lived near Inverness at Cradle Hall, so called from a contraption into which the first guest overcome with liquor could be placed and hoisted up above the dining-room table – his convivial hospitality was still a byword when I was a girl. The 'Highland Lady' in her *Memoirs* highly praised his improvements at the Slochd. She wrote 'A new road has been engineered along the sides of Slochd Mor; thought a wonder of skill beside the narrow precipitous pathway tracked out by General Wade.'[11] North of the Slochd Caulfeild's road has largely been obliterated by other work but it joined Wade's road before the Findhorn where a bridge had been built about 1760. I like to imagine that the attractive bit of grass-grown road through the birch wood at Soilshan is part of his road. A little after his time the approach to the Slochd from Strath Spey and the South was changed and the road was diverted to go through Carrbridge.

The military roads had been built because of the danger of an armed Jacobite rising in the Highlands. After Culloden this danger no longer existed and the roads had become more and more out of date. They had not been constructed to carry the increasingly heavy civilian traffic. The military funds available and the old Scots system of keeping the roads in repair by 'Statute Labour', i.e. by unpaid work on the roads for a specified number of days (generally three) by the people living by the road, were inadequate to maintain and improve them.[12] In addition, in

Joseph Mitchell. Portrait in the Town House Inverness.

order to take the more direct route to their objective, the roads had some very steep gradients.

It was the wish to avoid the long and steep gradients on Wade's road where it crossed Strath Nairn through the pass of the Threshold of the Highlands and by the bridge at Faillie, that eventually led to the making of the road south of Moy, as I know it, and as it has remained until the construction of the very newest road. It was planned to take the road through a gap in the hills to the east of that used by Wade and to cross the Nairn at Craggie, a point where the sides of the Strath have become lower and less steep. There were many difficulties, especially that of providing the necessary funds, and the plans hung fire for many years.

Then, in 1801, new factors came into play. There had been acute distress in many parts of the Highlands, especially in the North and West and the authorities commissioned Thomas Telford to plan and carry out an extensive scheme to alleviate the poverty and develop the economic potential of the Highlands.

Telford's plans included the construction of the Caledonian Canal, the building of a number of harbours and the improvement of the system of Highland roads. Parliament voted funds and appointed a Commission for the Care of the Parliamentary Roads. Under the auspices of this Commission work quickly started on the new section of the road, which in 1807 was approved by Telford. The roads under the care of the Commissioners were referred to as 'The Parliamentary Roads'. For easy reference I will call this particular bit of the road by this name. The rest of the road as I knew it, was also a Parliamentary Road, but the project was carried through by a most outstanding man about fifty years later and I always associate it with his name.

Two men, father and son, succeeded each other as Senior Inspector of Roads under the Commissioners and gave devoted service. Fortunately, the diary of the son, Joseph Mitchell, has been published as *Reminiscences of my Life in the Highlands*. It enables one to picture that sturdy figure walking, riding, driving 9500 miles a year in his endless odyssey to maintain, improve and extend the roads. He remade the road through the Slochd for the third time and then diverted the line of the road westwards, crossing the Findhorn about a mile above Wade's crossing. His bridge was replaced by a hideous one when the road was resurfaced in the 1920s. Mitchell's new bit of the road then gradually rose to higher ground and the modern village of Tomatin has developed near it. Further on, near Dalmagarry, his new road followed almost the same line as

Wade's road, actually covering it most of the time. Later on, the railway was also to go much the same way. Near Moy, Mitchell's road joined the section of Parliamentary Road that had already been made and the military roads were entirely superceded. He also suggested the making of a road connecting Deeside and Strath Spey by way of Glen Feshie, a project the possibilities of which have continued to be discussed all through my life.

Mitchell had already, in the 1840s, become deeply interested in the great innovation of building railway lines through the Highlands. The project aroused much opposition because Aberdeen was already connected with the South by the North of Scotland Railway, the Directors of which resented any invasion of potential spheres of development. A beginning was made in 1855 when a line was opened between Inverness and Nairn; this was extended in 1858 to join a line between Aberdeen and Keith. It was known as the Inverness and Aberdeen Junction Railway.[13]

Mitchell, however, as early as 1845, had had the ambitious idea of a direct line between Inverness and Perth. Himself an Inverness man, he had the enthusiastic backing of the whole community and two local men, Aeneas Mackintosh of Raigmore, whose disreputable kinsman we have already met, and Colonel Fraser Tytler of Aldourie, were his influential backers. Mackintosh of Mackintosh was one of the two lairds who, at one time, offered to give free passage through their land for the line.[14]

His original plan was for the line to run via Dunkeld and Drumochter and then, following a different route to that taken by the road, to Inverness. This plan met with opposition but, after many disappointments, at last, in 1861, part of his plan was realized and an Act was passed authorizing the construction of a railway line from Dunkeld, over Drumochter and down the Spey Valley to Forres, already a station on the existing line between Inverness and Keith. This line, the Inverness and Perth Junction Railway, was successfully constructed and opened in 1863 and, in due course, the Highland Railway was born.[15]

This was the position as I remember hearing it from my grandparents. There was no through service beyond Perth and generally a long wait. There were, however, pleasant memories of this. In the closely knit Highland society of those days there were meetings between friends and neighbours who were travelling, and delicious meals, served in Perth Station Restaurant with a vase of flowers on each table, were catered for by a firm named Peacock – the name stuck in my childish memory.

Last working appearance of a Highland Railway Engine built in 1894. Photograph by George Dixon.

Ninety years hence, one doubts if the excellence of the present catering of British Rail will be a happy memory.

To reach Strathdearn my mother's parents left the train and drove from Boat of Garten. But carriers from Inverness served the Strath and some years ago I met the daughter of the last of them, a very old woman. For passengers from Inverness to Tomatin there was a mail gig. My mother remembered that, at the top of the hill down to the Nairn, the able-bodied passengers were expected to get out, go straight down the steep slope by a footpath, climb the opposite side and rejoin the mail gig, which had followed the longer road, at the top. A few years ago the foot-path that they went by was still visible. If a good-natured piper or fiddler were among them he might give them a tune.

It was not till the 1890s that Joseph Mitchell's old dream was fulfilled and the direct railway line between Aviemore and Inverness was constructed. It was a costly and ambitious project. Extensive engineering work was required at the Slochd. Then there was the viaduct over the Findhorn not far from Wade's old ford. I can just remember the view up the Strath before the viaduct was built, and I think that it has been an improvement and seems to hold the prospect together.

After Moy the railway and the road part company and the former crosses the valley of the Nairn by yet another viaduct.

The coming of the railway in that pre-automobile age made a great difference to the amenities of living in Strathdearn and yet made no invasion on its privacy. The Highland Railway had been founded by local enterprise and there continued to be a strong feeling of attachment to it by the community. It was a pleasure to recognize the moss-green carriages and to know that every engine bore a Highland name.

Its proverbial unpunctuality was excused as one would some idiosyncracy of a valued friend. If one were travelling on the line via Nairn and Forres, where trains were more frequent, there was always the chance of getting the previous train as a delightful bonus. At Tomatin travellers were not left on the bleak platform or forced to shelter in the chilly waiting-room, but were welcomed into the friendly atmosphere and the warmth of a glorious fire in the Station-Master's room. That was only one instance of the personal kindness of the staff, instances of which any regular traveller on the line must remember. My particular one was the kindness and sympathy of the Station Master when I knocked him up one night to ask him to let me use the railway telephone to make an urgent call to Inverness and the nearest doctor. The road was rough and

The Slochd showing cuttings for road and rail.

The Railway viaduct across the Findhorn. Photographs by George Dixon.

dark and had seemed interminably long that night and the station telephone was the only one within reach.

The railway, like the whole district, reached its highest peak of activity every August. The trains became crowded with staff and then with sporting tenants and their guests as every shooting lodge and big house filled up with shooting parties for the 'Glorious Twelfth'. The platforms were thronged with men in sporting wear with gun-cases, the luggage vans with gun dogs and the great domed trunks into which ladies' maids packed Victorian finery.

Outside the station there was quite a bustle of traffic on the roads. For a considerable section of the community, the lairds who depended on the shooting rents, the keepers and the ghillies and many other people employed about the estate, it was the beginning of the few weeks upon which their incomes depended. For the rather miscellaneous assortment of people who would be employed as beaters it meant extra cash for a few weeks. The six to eight weeks of activity were a welcome break for everyone and people took a kindly interest in the 'bags' on the different moors. Then, as the days began to draw in and the autumn tints of rowan, birch and bracken began to glow, the shooting lodges emptied, the train was crowded with passengers for the South and the Strath relapsed into its usual quiescence.

Within my own personal experience, the Highland Railway reached one of its most distinctive moments when, in 1906, a special train was run from Inverness to Moy to convey guests to the ball that was one of the Coming-of-Age celebrations for Angus, only son and heir to Mackintosh of Mackintosh. Friends and kinsfolk had driven in their carriages into Inverness or come there by train. The platform was crowded with women, their best evening finery muffled up in silken cloaks and wraps, and men in full Highland dress. It was the culminating point of an epoch. Less than a decade later, the First World War was to take its toll of all too many of the men who had danced at that ball, Angus Mackintosh among them. They included members of the leading families of that part of the Highlands and it is sad to think how many of these have died out or sold their land.

Methods of transport have changed. Nowadays the hiring of a special train to take people the dozen or so miles from Inverness to Moy for a ball and back would be an anachronism. The economic structure of society has been reorientated and in 1923 the Highland Railway became part of the London Midland and Scottish Railway, (a grouping of railway lines) although, until 1942, it kept some of its own identity.[16]

Meanwhile it was the rapid increase in motor transport that led to a final alteration in the old road which by now had come under the care of Inverness County Council. In the early 1920s, under a comprehensive scheme for the improvement of Highland roads, it was widened and resurfaced. An awkward bend at the Slochd was improved and so were some of the many blind corners along it. Concrete replaced masonry in the making of the unattractive-looking bridge and the culverts which, to my mind, seemed to have a look of Rennie Mackintosh about their designs.

The most significant thing about the road, however, is the complete change in methods of construction, between those still used in the reconstructions of the twenties, and those in use upon the new road now being made. The labour of constructing it was done by a gang of navvies whose behaviour was a constant topic of conversation among the local people. The heavy labour on the new road is done by special machines controlled by a small number of skilled men. It is pleasant to think of the greater comfort and privacy that they enjoy in their private caravans or by being able to drive home from work in their cars, but there is the nagging thought that the displacement of human labour by that of machines is beginning to pose a serious social and economic problem.

The end of the dozen or so miles of the A9 that I am writing about happens to coincide, when one looks back, with a social landmark. The formal opening of a section of the road by Mrs Mackintosh of Mackintosh, wife of the Chairman of Inverness County Council, was recorded on a stone beside the road.

2

Railway to River

To return from my long digression from the Slochd – the next bit of the road as I knew it was that stretch engineered by Joseph Mitchell. It crossed the ridge of the Monadh Liath by the easiest gradient and, avoiding the steep descent to the Findhorn made by Wade's road and the use of the vastly costly viaducts constructed for the railway and for the new road, it used the more gentle descent of the shallow glen higher up the river. Mitchell wrote with some satisfaction over this detour, planned to turn the destruction of the bridge in the Moray Floods of 1829 to good account. It was made at a cost of from £7000 to £8000.[1]

It is not often that the stories about the men who actually worked on the road survive but, when a man named Alexander Mackintosh succeeded to the farm of Balgordonach, he found that there was a heavy debt on it. To earn money to save it he worked with his horse and cart in making the embankment and lived on '21 broses a week' – and paid off the debt. He must have been a character. In his old age he went into Inverness one day just when the stooks were standing in the field. It was a fine day and, as it is vitally important to 'lead' the corn to the stackyard and build the sheaves into stacks while it is perfectly dry (otherwise the straw will heat and be ruined), his sons and servants led the corn without his orders. When he got home he was furious and had every sheaf taken back to the field and re-stooked!

In my youth a man said that he used to see fairies in this little glen of the Allt Cosachd and that once, in play, they had snatched the cap off his head. This is an instance of how popular ideas have replaced local folklore for, in the old days, it used to be more politic to refer to such beings as 'Men of Peace' or the 'Good Folk' and they are very different to the tiny gauzy-winged sprites that tended white foxgloves in English gardens. There is good reason for believing J.F. Campbell's theory that

Making Wade's Road. By Paul Sandby, National Gallery of Scotland.

stories about fairies are relics of ancient traditions, especially of prehistoric people or strangers. Very often such stories are told about places with prehistoric remains. In this case, close to the farm of Drumbain, on the top of the slope on the right hand of the glen, early earthen ramparts can still be seen and there are other associations with the remote past.[2] The *Old Statistical Account* mentions a 'Great Circle of Death', apparently very near where Wade's road descends to the Findhorn, but it has entirely disappeared and there is not even a local tradition about it. It has been suggested that possibly it was a Clava type of cairn.[3] I gather that the Bronze Age, to which many remains go back, can be dated 1900 BC in Scotland. Remains of a settlement classified as a Bronze Age village were identified on the slope of the hill and there were other traces of prehistoric habitation, many damaged by the making of the successive roads, especially the newest one. Close by there are also two interesting place-names. To the left, beyond Drumbain, was the old estate of Raigmore = *Relig Mor* = Big Burying Place. To the right, a group of cottages on the slope by Wade's road is called Raigbeg = *Relig Beg* = Little Burying Place, but at neither of these places is there any remains of a graveyard.

The lie of the land is very suitable for an early settlement. Sir Aeneas Mackintosh of Mackintosh, who so acutely noticed every detail in his beloved Strath, wrote that all the plain (i.e. the flat middle of the strath) was once bog or wooded swamp and was only gradually cleared and drained and that the people formerly lived on and cultivated the sides of the mountain.[4] Actually there is a distinct shelf of good land along the sides of the hills that is still cultivated as parts of the farms of Corriebrough, Drumbain and Clune. As an interesting parallel, Forsyth, who wrote so fully about Strath Spey, noticed the same sort of thing on the other side of the Monadh Liath.[5] One is very acutely aware of the continuity of human life when one thinks of all the chances and changes through which men have cultivated their land, from the time of the Bronze Age folk with their strange preoccupation with memorials to the dead, and that of the mysterious Picts, to the warfare and raiding of the clans and, at last, to the evolution of modern life.

Even earlier than this settlement, near the farm of Balmore, on the floor of the Strath, small hut circles have been discovered with traces of small areas of land that had once been cultivated. I am indebted to Mr J.G. Dunbar, the Secretary of the Royal Commission on Ancient Monuments, for the information that the remains of similar hut circles had been found in the rich agricultural district round Nairn and that they had been attributed to the third millennium BC. No one knows what happened to these people or if they are in any way connected with later inhabitants. Were they so prosperous that they spread even to so remote a spot as Strathdearn, or were they forced to retreat before the spread of a more formidable people? Is it some faint memory of them, or of their successors, that lingered on preserved in tales, becoming ever more vague and distorted, and in place-names? About halfway across the Strath, between the two groups of hut circles, but also near to a Pictish relic, there is the Fairy Hill. A few miles up the Strath, at Dalarossie, there is a standing stone with a hole in it and I understand that other archaeological remains have been found; yet further up, there is an area that is now generally known as the Coigs – the Fifths – but at least as late as the seventeenth century was called Schephin – the Land of Peace or Fairy Land.

The names of the five Coigs were:

Coignascalen – Place of the tents or huts
Coignafinternach – Place where the smith worked
Coignavullin – Place of the mill
Coignashee – Place of the fairies
Coignafearn – Place of the alders[6]

By the time of written records of the past the Coigs were used as shielings by some of the farmers of Badenoch (the upper part of Strath Spey). It is easy to picture a small isolated community, the last refuge of a vanishing society, visited in the summer by herdsmen from a more accessible part of the country. Highland folk were told of other beings: Gruagachs, Glaistigs and Brownies, probably stories of individuals of an earlier race who survived either as wild or semi-wild beings like the Glaistigs and Gruagachs or domesticated into individual families of the succeeding race like the Brownies. I like to imagine that as the way of life of the Scots gradually replaced that of the Picts – the latter were quite strong in parts of North-Eastern Scotland so late as the eleventh century – the little community at the head of Strathdearn was a last pocket of the Pictish language, manners and customs.

Returning to memories directly associated with our bit of the road, I was told that the slope on the left at the entrance to our little glen was the place where, at Easter time, eggs were rolled down the hill in order to foretell the future. This, of course, was the survival of a pagan rite adapted to Christian belief.

I do not think that the Gospel came the way of the Slochd, but by a well-known route over the hills much further up the Strath. Dalarossie, the Meadow of Fergus, was already a settlement when St Fergus himself or, more probably one of his followers, founded the church there. The name of the Aberdeenshire village of St Fergus is only one of the sites there (and also in far off Caithness) that bears his name. In his labours he was closely associated with St Drostan, St Medan, St Colm (or Colman) and with St Ternan. St Ternan was particularly venerated at Banchory Ternan on the Dee and, from upper Deeside to the upper valley of the Spey, the Cairngorms can easily be crossed by the Lairig Ghru and by Glen Feshie. Almost opposite the latter there is Dunachton, where the ruined chapel was dedicated to St Ternan and, from there, there is a hill track constantly used by my great-great-great-grandfather and his son when they farmed Dunachton in Strath Spey and Clune in Strathdearn. Dr Douglas Simpson worked out a fascinating picture of the evangelization of the North-East, from Aberdeenshire to Angus, by a great missionary group, and its relation to the art and social structure of the Picts. He traces its origin to Candida Casa and its founder St Ninian who, at the end of the fourth century, was the earliest apostle to Scotland.[7] This, however, is a theory that can be challenged and a Columban and Irish origin can be claimed for St Fergus and St Ternan.[8] Wherever they came from, in essential beliefs not only were the followers of St Columba and St Ninian at one, although there were some individual customs in the Columban Church, but they were also in communion with the rest of the Western Church. It is significant that, in the Service Book from the ancient monastery of Deer in Aberdeenshire, a rubric in Gaelic added to the Latin service for the Visitation of the Sick should contain the words: 'Here hand him the Sacrifice.'

The church at Dalarossie must have been used as a mission. We do not know how this was organized or for how long. The early building has disappeared, the only possible relic being a primitive font formed out of a hollowed stone, but the tradition of its holiness persisted in the belief that no evil thing would enter that sacred ground. There is a terrible story that a herdsman going from Badenoch to Dalarossie was overtaken by a desperately hurrying woman. It was the Witch of Laggan fleeing to Dalarossie for sanctuary from the devil. Shortly afterwards the herdsman was overtaken by a black man on a black horse followed by two black hounds and, still later, he met them returning with the body of the woman lying across the saddlebow of the horse.

Dalarossie Church on the banks of the Findhorn. Photograph by George Dixon.

Eventually in the thirteenth century, in the organization of the whole church in Scotland, Dalarossie was made into a prebend of Elgin Cathedral although, apparently from almost the first, it was served by the same priest as Moy. The present building dates from 1790.[9]

The focus of interest in the Strath by that time had shifted much further down the river to Moy and it is easier to visualize the effects of great changes further along the road but, at this point in our journey, following the road down this little glen, there is one association that helps one to appreciate the enormous change that took place in the religious life of the community.

At Drumbain Farm, as I have mentioned, there are some prehistoric earthworks. I was told that it used to be customary to bury there the bodies of babies who had not been christened before they died. What tragedies must have hung about that place. It was the custom in the Church of Scotland to refuse to baptize an illegitimate child until the name of the father had been disclosed so that he might be made to do public penance. Although this was certainly the case in Strathdearn in the eighteenth century, I think and hope that the severer measure of refusing all help to the unhappy girl if she did not tell the name of her seducer, was never practised there. What betrayal and humiliation these women must have felt, besides the grief of a mother mourning the loss of a child that she believed had been denied eternal felicity.

One of the strangest things about the story of Strathdearn is the way in which its people, who enjoyed their pleasures very robustly and whom history shows to have been high-spirited and intransigent, should not only have accepted, but wholeheartedly embraced, an exceptionally austere form of religious practice and become 'one of the most intensely Puritan districts in the north'.[10] At the time of the reforms after the Reformation, Mackintosh of Mackintosh was sympathetic to the new church but, during the sixteenth century, the church suffered acutely from shortage of ministers − for instance in 1574 there was only one minister for the care of Moy, Dalarossie, Boleskine, Daviot and Dores.[11] And Mackintosh of Mackintosh and his clan, with the exception of that one brief evangelical phase at the time of the Reformation, were Royalist and then Jacobite in sympathies. The Rev. Alexander Cumming, who was minister from 1680 to 1709, was a strong Jacobite although he was not actually displaced as a non-juror.[12] Jacobitism and Episcopalianism often went together and Strathdearn, in the early eighteenth century, was described as 'a hotbed of Episcopalianism'.

For several years the parishes of Moy and Dalarossie were vacant. Then, in 1716, the Rev. James Leslie was appointed. It was his first charge and he was not made welcome. It was, of course, at the time when the people of Strathdearn were suffering for the part that they had taken in the Rising of the '15. Mackintosh himself was still in prison. Mr Leslie's induction at the kirk at Moy was attended by a large number of ministers and by Rose of Kilravock and Campbell of Cawdor, two influential men in the North. Trouble was apparently expected, but the ceremony went off peacefully. It was a different matter up the glen. The first time he went to preach at Dalarossie he was accosted at Kyllachie, while on his way, by a group of women with their aprons full of stones. He called out, 'Let the woman who is the biggest witch among you throw the first stone.' None of the women would so identify herself and he was allowed to pass.

When he got to Dalarossie he found that the local men were amusing themselves by the old Highland pastime of 'putting the stone', i.e. seeing who could throw or move a large natural boulder, which was called the *Clach Neart* = stone of strength. (In my youth the Moy *Clach Neart* was preserved at the front door of the old Moy Hall.) They were unwilling to stop playing and come to church, so he struck a bargain with them that, if he were able to throw the stone further than any of them, they would come into the church and hear him. Being a man of exceptional strength he did so, and they kept to the agreement.

There are tales of his unusual strength as, for instance, when he found the narrow track along the cliff face at the Streens blocked by a pony; he simply lifted it out of the way. A story that does him infinite credit happened in 1746. Mackintosh's wife, popularly known as 'Colonel Anne', was an ardent Jacobite and raised the clan to fight for Prince Charles Edward. Her politics must have been entirely opposed to his, yet when, after the disaster of Culloden, a party of undisciplined soldiers forced their way into Moy Hall and plundered her possessions, insulted her and threatened her with physical violence, Leslie, who was at the time in his later middle age, and happened to be on the other side of the Findhorn, immediately waded across and hurried to Moy Hall to do his best to protect her. Fortunately, disciplined troops under proper control arrived very soon afterwards.[13]

He was energetic in organizing his parish. He is said to have appointed twenty-two elders in one day, and the Parish Register, which (with a tactful blank for 1745) still exists, is the chronicle of an active but austere religious life. During his ministry the parish church of Moy was rebuilt (in 1765). He died in 1766 and was buried there. It is strange that after a ministry of fifty years no tombstone was erected to his memory. The significant fact of his ministry is that the people had come not merely to submit to, or accept, but to welcome a severe form of religious practice. In a number of Highland parishes, by the late eighteenth century, groups of individuals known as 'the Men' had grown up. They had no official status in the Church. I have never learnt how they were chosen or assumed membership of the group. They visited, admonished and criticized anything that infringed their rigid evangelical standards. In many parishes they presumed to find fault with the minister if he did not conform to their exacting standards. In Strathdearn the 'Five Godly Donalds' flourished about the same time as the Rev. James Leslie, or rather later, but I never heard that they presumed to come into collision with him. I suspect that, had they done so, the reverberations would have resounded down the centuries. There was not, however, a rapid and complete alteration in the social life of the district. In 1794 the local minister reported of his congregation that: 'In their manners, they are remarkably attached to old customs and practices. The language, dress and most of the peculiarities of the old Highlanders continue in this place, with very little alteration. Excepting the gentry few of the inhabitants of this place speak English nor do they discover much inclination to acquire that language.'[14]

It is necessary to retail a little ecclesiastical history in order to understand local developments. The emergence of an evangelical movement is, of course, part of the general history of the Church at this time. A strong wave of sectarianism reached Strathdearn from the neighbouring straths of the Spey and the Nairn and the rigidly puritanical sect 'the Seceders' found many supporters.[15]

It is not therefore surprising that, when a great rift within the Church of Scotland began to develop, very strong feelings were aroused in Strathdearn. There was an acute difference in the general attitudes and views of the opposing sides, so aptly termed the 'High Flyers' and the 'Grey Egyptians' — charity is not a characteristic of the unco' guid. The immediate point upon which the conflict took place was the right to appoint a new minister when a parish fell vacant. This had been a matter of recurrent debate since the Church was established and the rights of patronage of the heritors was several times abolished and then restored. Finally, in 1843, the breaking point was reached and the Moderator of the

General Assembly formally left it and was followed by about a third of the members.[16] They proceeded to form the Free Church which, without either the funds or the buildings of the established Church, set out to fulfil an equally wide ministry.

The minister of Moy was not among those who left the Church, but supporters of the Disruption were anxious to set up a kirk and minister of their own. In these days of an ecumenicalism which is often rather hazy about the Articles of Faith that are involved, it is difficult to realize the fervour and bitterness of polemics that still were violent and shocking even three-quarters of a century later when I, as a girl, can remember them. At the actual time of the Disruption there was also a very strong element of political feeling and the supporters of the new movement found difficulty in obtaining land from the landlords upon which to build their new church and manse.

During my uncle Canon Mackintosh's lifetime, the elders of the parish came to ask him for a little more land to improve the access. He used to tell us that they had told him that, at the time when the original request for land had been made to my grandfather, he had been obliged to go to India to earn money as an indigo planter in order to save the estate. He had still been doubtful if he would be able to free it from its encumbrances, and he had said that he would give them the land and that, if he lost his estate, he would be glad to think that the last thing he did with it was to give some of it for God's purposes. One of the elders had replied that he would not lose his land and his son would inherit it after him. As a matter of fact his great-grandson still has a part of it.

It must have been with infinite self-sacrifice that the new struggling community built the present comely church on the land beside the road at this point and the manse on the other side.

As a collector of old traditions and stories one is inclined to blame 'Scottish Calvinism' for the destruction of so much of the great heritage of tradition, poetry and music that brought joy into the lives of the people. It is interesting to try to assess the extent and the causes of this loss to the people of Strathdearn.

In the first place I would like to record my immense debt to Mr Davidson and other older members of the community for all they told me of the old ways of agriculture and of the daily surroundings of the people's lives. What little I have passed on in writing, and in forming the Folk Museum, widens the debt to them.

I do not know if it is by chance or old religious prejudice but there seem to be fewer rowan trees planted about the farmhouses in Strathdearn than in nearby districts. One always imagines that at least the older rowan trees were planted to safe-guard the place from witches.

Of course one knows that in certain families music and literature were actively discouraged but, by and large, one is left with the impression that it is the country people who have themselves allowed their inheritance of Gaelic literature, music and tradition to die from inanition – simply by failing to keep it alive. To take an illustration from elsewhere, one sees, from Miss Bassin's book on Frances Tolmie,[17] how the cycle of songs associated with the fulling of the cloth went out of use around the more sophisticated Portree, although they were still being sung at Dunvegan.

In Strathdearn there is evidence that, at one time, people were familiar with the great epics of Gaeldom. One of the best-known stories in the group, known as the Ultonian Cycle, is that of Deirdre of the Sorrows. Shorn of the delicacy and subtlety of the delineation, the imagery of the description and the crescendo of tragedy in the original telling of the story, its bare outlines are that Conchobar, King of Ulster, intended to marry his beautiful ward Deirdre. But she saw and fell in love with Naoise and, accompanied by his two brothers, the lovers fled to Alba. King Conchobar lured them back with promises of pardon and friendship which Deirdre disbelieved. The three brothers were killed and, to prevent Conchobar from marrying her, Deirdre killed herself. The story survived in Barra in oral tradition till Carmichael took it down. According to the oral version of it in Lorn, Deirdre's dwelling place when she fled to Scotland was on Loch Etive, but so well and widely was the tale known that it was also localized in Glen Farigaig on the southern side of Loch Ness.

The head waters of the Nairn and of the Farigaig are close together. Strath Nairn was largely inhabited by branches of Clan Chattan, the firm allies of the Mackintoshes, and there was a close connection between the upper parts of Strath Nairn and Strathdearn; one may feel sure that the story was well known in both straths. I may add that Strath Nairn did not undergo the same puritanical revival as the following tale illustrates.

I was told that someone at Drynachan, some miles down the Streens, had some old stories and I went to see her. She said that she was sorry to have to tell me that the people of Strath Nairn had been very wicked.

Eager for some lurid yarn of ill-doing, I asked what they had done. She replied that a godly minister had come to preach to them and that they had rabbled him. 'But,' she added darkly, 'they have their punishment yet'. I knew that fire and brimstone had not fallen on Strath Nairn but, expectantly, I asked what it was. 'They still have a great many Episcopalians among them,' she said gloomily. Being an Episcopalian, I am afraid that I allowed some faint trace of the amusement that I felt to show on my face. For an instant she showed consternation at having been unwittingly discourteous to a guest. Then, with the complete social adequacy so characteristic of Highland country people, she returned my grin and we both laughed. In spite of this, people knowledgeable of the district seemed to know nothing of the story.

I actually happened to go to see Dun Dearduil in Glen Farigaig. A friend born and bred in the district took me. It is a lovely glen. In the middle of it a pinnacle of rock has broken away from one steep side of the glen and the Farigaig swirls round its foot. It is a place of obvious strength and a vitrified fort is built on the top. The following conversation took place:

Hester: 'That rock is called Dunyardle. That means Deirdre's Dun. It doesn't sound like that, but that's to do with Gaelic spelling and pronunciation.'

I agreed.

Hester: 'There's an old story about it. Deirdre was supposed to be able to catch salmon out of her window. She would need a line thirty or forty feet long and of course a proper rod and reel and I doubt if there were such things in her day. If we scramble up you can have a look.'

We scrambled up.

Hester: 'If you leant a bit further over and held out this stick and had a line with a weight on it, you could drop it into the pool below.'

Myself: 'Thanks awfully. I'll take the story's word for it.'

The small incident that salmon could be caught from Deirdre's refuge actually occurs in the story and it seems to have caught the public imagination. In Strath Spey, on the other side of Strathdearn, in a fictitious tale about the origin of the Grants, the ancestress was said to be a lady named Bigla. The site of her castle, also a natural stronghold, is still pointed out and she was said to have been able to catch salmon in a net from it. Perhaps Deirdre used one too.

The second cycle of Gaelic epics consisted of stories about the Feinné, and their leader, Finn MacCoul. The Feinné were a band of warriors who defended Gaeldom against the attacks of the Lochlannach. The main tales originated in Eire but took root in Alba. More and more stories about the doings of the Feinné were added but the distinctive characteristics of the different heroes were preserved – the wisdom (not to say cunning) of Finn, the impetuous bravery of Osgar, the swift-footedness of the ever-willing Caoilte, the truculence of the surly Goll, the charm of Diarmid and his fatal attraction for women that was to lead to the most tragic tale, and so on with the special qualities of many others of the band.

In the Western Highlands several of the stories were localized. In Perthshire, as we know from Stewart of Garth, the doings of the Feinné were the main topics of conversation among the people; but it was in Badenoch that James Macpherson grew up hearing the stories that he was to 'translate' – transmogrify into the gloomy magniloquence of his 'Ossian'.

Of course, they must also have been told in Strathdearn and, when I pressed them, two of the older men told me that they had heard of Finn and some of the other characters in their youth, but that such stories had been regarded as unprofitable. In Dr Thomas Sinton's collection of *The Poetry of Badenoch* there is a rather late and sophisticated poem, a lament for my great-grandfather, in which the writer likens himself to Oisin mourning the dead members of the Feinné; the blood of Finn himself was said to have 'formed a living lining' to 'the clay' of the departed. The only point about this poem that my family remembered was the achievement of the deceased as a sportsman. Sir Aeneas Mackintosh wrote, at the end of the eighteenth century, that the country people would spend the evening telling stories of 'ghosts and hobgoblens, every word of which they believe'.

There is now a lack of stories of the supernatural. Witches surely were respectable subjects – was there not the Witch of Endor? – but even a story about MacQueen of Pollochaig, which I shall relate later, seems to be forgotten. Ghosts are not a frivolous subject and, as a child, I was told that sometimes a white lady had been seen on the hillside above Pollochaig, but that to do so was a sure sign of death.

The only case of second sight connected with Strathdearn happened to someone whose family had long before emigrated to Canada. Her family had kept in touch with my uncle and I met her when she came to London. In the course of a general conversation she said that, sometimes, she had the strange experience of seeing a grey mist round people – often strangers in the street – and that the feeling was specially distasteful when it was wrapped close round their chests. I exclaimed, 'But that is the Winding Sheet! You have second sight!'

She was much interested and recalled that she had been on a visit to this country in the spring of 1914. A cousin's regiment happened to be quartered at Dover and he had written to her saying that he hoped to be in London for a day and asking her to go out with him. When they met he said that the first thing to do was to cash a cheque at Cox's (then the bank most used by officers). When they got there the place was full of young men, some of them brother officers of her cousin, and suddenly she saw, round a great many of them, the grey mist that she dreaded. She felt faint and was much embarrassed at what she thought a silly weakness. Her cousin's regiment was in the retreat from Mons in August 1914 and all his brother officers round whom she had seen the mist were killed. Of course, many of the other young soldiers she had seen at Cox's that day must also have been among the terrible casualties of the 1914 War – the Lost Generation.

There are so many place-names containing the word fairy that it is only natural that people should have some ideas about such beings, but such scraps as I have heard are very trivial and are obviously derived from conventional story-book ideas, much as the tale of the fairies I have already told. They are very different to the tales of the formidable *Sithe* of Gaelic tradition. I have never heard a local story of a changeling or of the adventure of a human being in a Fairy Dun. No doubt such stories once existed. There was a grand Strath Nairn one that partly took place in Strathdearn and at the appropriate spot I shall hope to tell it.

Like most places Strathdearn had a buried treasure. Mr MacAskill has most kindly put the tale in English rhyme for me:

On Tomnahully old folks say,
That the New Year's earliest ray
Of sunlight strikes a certain stone,
Which has since olden times lain on
A golden treasure wrapped within
The cover of a young foal's skin.

Murdo MacAskill. His father, Donald, had the traditional Gaelic gift of expressing himself in poetry which he has inherited.

In spite of the lack of the usual minatory clause to the finder, the treasure has so far been undiscovered!

Strath Spey has a considerable part, if not one of the greatest, in the flowering of Gaelic poetry that was called forth by the Jacobite movement. To be honest, I have heard more of Colonel John Roy Stewart's exciting adventures than of his poetry. Born and bred in Strath Spey he was a close and adoring associate of Prince Charles Edward, served with great distinction during the '45 and then spent a long time as a fugitive in Strath Spey with many exciting adventures, before escaping to France where he died. He must have had close friendships in Strathdearn, for among his poems – which range from passionate Jacobite laments to quite light-hearted songs – is a lament for Lady Mackintosh (not 'Colonel Anne' but her predecessor).[18] The names of more than half a dozen other Strath Spey poets are recorded, but one gets closer to everyday people in Dr Thomas Sinton's *The Poetry of Badenoch*, which indeed bears out Mrs Grant of Laggan's statement that 'in every cottage there is a musician and in every hamlet a poet'. The poetry Dr Sinton records is that of the people. It expresses, in many cases in local settings, every mood of life, sad and joyful. There are laments, love-songs, humourous and satirical rhymes, rhythmic verses for reaping and ploughing and a very large number of devotional poems. So closely were Badenoch and Strathdearn linked that one may feel sure that this heritage of poetry was shared. In both districts, poetry as a vehicle of everyday expression seems to have died out before the general use of Gaelic, its vehicle, but we, in Strathdearn, may feel proud that we can boast of our own poet in the person of Donald MacAskill whose son has helped me so greatly in my remembrances of the road.

In the old days a marked Highland talent was a facility for improvising verse. There is no surviving story of such improvisation by any one native to the Strath, but a tale has been cherished about a complete stranger – the Earl of Mar.

The Earls of Mar were great magnates during one period of Highland history. Earl Alexander commanded the royal army at Harlaw and also at the first Battle of Inverlochy. All fought against the forces of the Lord of the Isles. In the first Battle of Inverlochy (1431) the Mackintoshes and Camerons were with the royal army which was roundly defeated.

The tale of Mar's escape was told locally in Lochaber, till within living memory, with very precise detail. Wandering alone, as a fugitive, through what is most aptly termed 'the Rough Bounds' he asked a poor

woman for a bite of food. She could only give him a little meal which he
mixed with water in the heel of his shoe and he said:—

> 'Is maith air còcaire an t-acras,
> Is mairg a ni taileas air biath:
> Fuarag iòrna à sàil mo bhròige
> Biadh as fheàrr a fhuair mi riamh'

> ('Hunger is a good food
> Pity him who would scorn food.
> Barley mixture from the heel of my shoe
> Is the best food I ever had')

Eventually he made his way up Glen Roy and over the ridge where
centuries later General Wade was to build his road, down Glen Tarff and
so to the Great Glen near what is now Fort Augustus. From there he
would easily have made his way among friendly clans to the Royal Castle
at Inverness. While in Glen Tarff a poor man killed his last cow in order
to fulfil the obligations of hospitality and feed a hungry traveller. On
leaving, Mar told him who he was and said that he would always be
welcome at his Castle of Kildrummy in Aberdeenshire. Later on the
Macdonalds found out that the man had sheltered their enemy. They
drove him out and the tale tells of his recognition and welcome by Mar at
Kildrummy.

Part of this strongly localised tale became assimilated into the folklore
of Strathdearn a long time ago. I came across a version of it as an ancient
local tale in an account written nearly two hundred and fifty years ago.
According to this local version it was in the Streens that Mar wandered
and received the meal from a man, not a woman, but made the same
verse of acknowledgement. In one version I have heard that this man
afterwards went to the earl's Castle and was recognized and welcomed.
One would think that the Streens were rather far off the probable line of
Mar's flight, but as an example of an ancient tradition and its transference, I feel grateful to Mr Jimmie Dunbar who preserved it and told it
to me in Strathdearn. The story is occasionally associated with the Earl of
Mar who led the Rising of 1715, but this event falls within the era of
well recorded history and would be impossible.

Of course, all the poetry was in Gaelic, the natural tongue of the
people. During my mother's lifetime and mine the speaking of it has
almost died out in Strathdearn. Long ago my grandfather was much

surprised to hear a farmer speak to his collie in English and was told: 'Och he would be altogether too wise if he had the Gaelic'. And later on my mother noticed how the parents and older members of a family would discourage the children from speaking Gaelic, not only because it got them into trouble at school and they thought it would disadvantage them in later life, but because they liked to have a private language of their own. The theory of the educational advantages of bilingualism was certainly not held in Strathdearn.

I remember how the country people spoke when I was young. It was, as we used to say, 'through the Gaelic'; and it was much subtler than modern talk and sometimes with a beautiful cadence of words. Speaking of a family connection, I was told: 'His worst enemy could not be saying that he was the first to leave a pleasant party.'

As a child, I admired an old cock grouse, with beautiful markings and legs as finely feathered as if with grey fur, but tough and sinewy after his long hard life on the hill. 'There's a grand bird to give to your friends,' said the keeper. In Strath Spey I was taken to see someone so old that she had been a servant to my great-grandmother, to whom she had been devoted, and she remembered my great-great-grandmother as a formidable old lady. She was eager to see if I resembled her 'dear Leddy' as she called my great-grandmother. Her eyesight was failing but I knelt in front of her and she peered into my face. She did not see the likeness she sought but she said: 'She has the old leddy's eyes, the sad grey eyes that can see the sorrows of the world through her own tears.' It was an apt description for someone who has spent a good deal of her life writing Highland history and collecting for a Folk Museum the relics of the penurious, hard lives of Highland people, and who, as a child, could remember the shock of the sudden rush of casualties in the Boer War and, as a grown-up, has lived through the devastation of two World Wars. Mr MacAskill has a story of a man who was mending a fence when an old neighbour happened to pass and annoyed him by his blether on better ways to do the job. He endured this for some time but finally said: 'Mr Macdonald, we would greatly appreciate the assistance of your absence.'

There must have been a great deal of singing in Strathdearn in the old days. Almost every traveller to the Highlands mentioned how the people sang both at work and play. *Crodh Chailein* was a universal milking song, for the cows were sung to to encourage them to let down their milk. Burt noticed how the ploughmen sang; he called it 'a hideous Irish noise' but he said that the horses would stop if it ceased. We older ones can remember the ploughmen whistling as they drove their long furrows in the days before the rattle of the tractor took over.

I think that tunes have a greater power of survival than verse. I am sure that *Songs of the North* did immense service in keeping traditional music alive. It was published in three volumes. I in 1885, II in 1895 and III in 1926, and was edited by Harold Boulton. The words were in English, with a Gaelic chorus where appropriate, and the piano accompaniments were simple. Like thousands of other families, as children we sang and loved them and through them expressed our appreciation of our Highland heritage. Later on came the Mod. Mrs Kennedy Fraser, Kenneth Macleod and Frances Tolmie, and a number of successors who have carried on the work. Unfortunately, in this corner of the Highlands, the words of our local songs remain silent and forgotten – only preserved in print, because no one has recorded the airs to which they were sung.

The minister of the parish, writing in the 1830s, noted that the wearing of the kilt had almost entirely disappeared. The Highland dress and the tartan had so much significance that its abandonment was surely an indication of how much the people had lost their sense of special identity.[19]

Strath Spey, however, has gained outstanding distinction for its fiddle music and, as its close neighbour, Strathdearn at one time was full of the gay rhythm of the reel and strathspey. The *clarsach* – harp – was the best-known musical instrument in the Highlands in the Middle Ages. But the viol became fashionable in the south. In 1659 the Laird of Grant employed both a harper and a violer.[20] Then the fiddle took its place. There were famous families of composers and players such as the Comyns and the Browns, and some of our greatest reel and strathspey tunes were written in Strath Spey. They remain as a living art, enjoyed by all ranks of society, and not as a folksy revival. To suit simpler needs they were easily adapted to playing on 'the box' (the melodeon).

The pipes were not as important in Strathdearn as was the fiddle. Mackintosh, like any other self-respecting chief from the sixteenth century onwards, had his piper. Sir Aeneas's piper had been trained by the MacCrimmons. Of course the most important occasion for his piping was to animate the clan in battle and play a lament on his master's last journey to the grave. It was also traditional that he should play to wake him up in the morning. Sir Aeneas writes that another of his duties was to enliven the work of the bands of reapers at harvest time.

Highland Dancing. By D. Allan, National Gallery of Scotland.

It was only natural that, in a district which echoed with the splendid rhythms of the tunes that were being composed and played, people should also excel in dancing to them.[21] James Robertson, who spent many summers walking in the Highlands, wrote of a wedding in Strathdearn in 1771: 'In dancing they use a great variety of steps which they adapt to the music so admirably and with such graceful agility as could hardly be surpassed even by the best taught dancers.'[22] They evidently danced some dances that have been forgotten. Sir Aeneas Mackintosh wrote that they often danced a dance for two 'with steps like a fandango'. He also mentions the custom of dancing at funerals, the nearest relative leading the first dance, and that at weddings they would hold a dance for more than one night.

Dancing was properly taught in Strathdearn when my mother was a child and a dancing master paid regular visits; the maids also had lessons. She was told that she ought to be able to do her steps on a space no bigger than the size of a peat. The men about the place also took great pride in their dancing and, even in their heavy working boots, could do the Fling and the Shuffle dexterously. When she was a girl the custom for the men to give off periodic shouts while dancing was just coming in. Formerly the dancers performed in silence and the elder men among the spectators occasionally cheered them on by a shout. My mother remembered her intense embarrassment when an old gentleman, who disapproved of innovation, remarked to her in a loud voice, 'Just hark at them yowling like a pack of curs'. She also remembered that the dancing of the eight-some reel was just being introduced at the balls of the Northern Meeting at Inverness from the Perthshire Ball.

When I was a child I remember how a well-known dancing master, a Mr Lowe, used to come to Inverness every year to give a course of dancing lessons. He demonstrated the steps while playing the tune on his fiddle and occasionally poking the toes of awkward pupils with his bow. Of course the boys were taught the Highland Fling, but very neatly. We girls learnt a variety of steps but all done in a very small space, the feet kept very close to the floor and, as a grown-up, it was easy to do them in a long skirt, perhaps raised decorously to show off an ankle.

We danced reels and strathspeys. Lowland Scots country dancing was so entirely unknown that at children's parties we had danced Sir Roger de Coverley or the Swedish Wedding Dance. There was one exception. At the balls at the Northern Meetings the Inverness Country Dance was performed once. Partners faced each other in a long line and, in turn, danced down the line setting to partners as they went. It was after the First World War that country dancing came into fashion at Highland dances. Mrs Grant of Rothiemurchus did a great deal in teaching them to local people. She had worked hard at learning them at meetings of the Country Dance Society and was very particular that they should be done correctly.

3

Over the River

Like Mitchell's road we come at last to the river. All authorities are agreed that 'Find' means white but, whereas some consider that 'Earn' is the name of a Gaelic goddess, Professor Watson derived it from Eire and wrote that its meaning was White Ireland; however, as Eire itself was called after the goddess the difference of opinion is not important!

Rising as it does in the hills, the Findhorn is very swift. Its volume varies greatly. After a spell of dry weather, between the shrunken pools, the water finds its way among the boulders and larger stones in its bed, and it is not difficult to choose a place where one can wade across it. But when there is rain in the hills the river swells quickly in volume. Burt described how he saw a party of Highlanders crossing the river. They formed themselves into a line with their arms over each other's shoulders, the weakest in the middle and the strongest at the end which opposed the current. He found their expression of dread and anxiety intensely moving as they struggled over the stony bed of the river.[1] Wade did not build a bridge when he made the road and there were many losses by drowning until a bridge was built by General Barrington in 1763.[2]

When the river is actually in spate there seems to be a fierce joy in the turgid, racing water and it gnaws savagely at the rising grounds that deflect its course. The greatest spate of all, the floods of 1829, were minutely recorded by Sir Thomas Dick Lauder in *An Account of the Great Floods of August 1829*. Phenomenally heavy rain upon the head waters of the Findhorn and the Dulnain also affected the Spey below where the latter joined it. Every bridge was swept away and enormous damage was done to property. Lives almost miraculously escaped. In Strathdearn rain fell from Monday morning till Tuesday afternoon, so heavily that it came in through the cracks in the window frames and under the doors. The

Looking across the Findhorn towards Corriebrough. Photograph by A. Adam.

ensuing spate swept away acres of the best alluvial land on the farms and entirely ruined one (Shannachie).[3]

I happened to be living at Balvraid, at the lower end of Strathdearn, in 1914 when there was a small cloudburst that gave me some idea of what these floods were like. The abnormal rain only lasted about two hours and only affected a small area which, however, covered the head waters of the local burn, the Bruachaig, and of the Baddengorm, the burn running down the opposite side of the hill. The rain came in through the window frames and under the door in the same way as Sir Thomas described. My brother, then a schoolboy, was fishing in the burn in the glen and he saw it coming down in a wall of water, the bodies of dead sheep being carried along in it. He ran for his life to the steep side of the glen. I hurried down to Balnespick to find out if the gardener's family was safe. The swollen burn was tawny in colour. It was coming down in waves in a way that I have never seen in an ordinary spate. Louder than the sound of the rushing water was that of the grinding stones and boulders. Water was pouring over the hillside across the road, in one place so deep and swift-running that I was nearly swept off my feet.

At Balnespick a number of fully grown trees had been swept away, the soil from the garden scoured out, and the end of the gardener's cottage broken so that water was swirling round the table in what had been the parlour. The Lodge itself is higher up and so, fortunately, the gardener's family was able to go there. The flooding waters left a wide track of stones across the fields and next year this was covered by a dense growth of buttercups which, when they flowered, made a golden track. It was, however, like fairy gold and soon faded leaving the stones on the ruined land.

On the other side of the hill, the Baddengorm did even more serious damage. The railway bridge collapsed just as a train was going over it, its foundations being swept away by the raging floods. One coach fell into the torrent and five passengers were killed and nine injured.[4]

There were other ways of crossing the river. I do not know when 'cradle' bridges were invented. There is, or was, a cradle bridge further down the river. It consisted of a wooden receptacle hung on a wire cable stretched between two posts, one on each side of the river. When the wire is taut it is easy to pull oneself across the river, hand over hand but, if the cable is slack, the cradle slides quickly to the lowest point above the middle of the river and it is hard work to haul it up to the further side. My mother and other people have told me that people used to cross the river on stilts but I have never seen it being done or even seen a pair of stilts at any of the houses.

After the Great Flood, Mitchell wrote that he felt like a doctor in an epidemic.[5] He set to work to replace all the bridges that had been destroyed but, with characteristic courage and devotion, he only made a temporary one for Wade's road and began the reconstruction of the road from the Slochd, making the diversion which became the permanent road (and which this account is following) and building a new bridge which was replaced when the road was resurfaced in the 1920s.

Salmon fishing is now preserved, but it is not particularly good. In the old days the river teemed with salmon. Mr Murdo MacAskill remembers being told that his grandmother, when a girl, got very tired of eating salmon roe when quantities of the spawning fish were caught in buckets in the mill lade and salted for winter eating. Smoked salmon was indeed an important item in the sparse winter diet as Sir Aeneas noted. The salmon were caught in nets or with coarse woollen flies or by damming a stream. None of these methods was illegal, but 'burning the water', holding a lighted torch over the water and spearing the fish as they were attracted to it, *was*.[6] The spear was known as a leister.

When I was collecting for Am Fasgadh at farms on other rivers besides the Findhorn, the following sort of conversation took place: 'I have in the barn a strange kind of a fork that you might care to have for your museum. It would not be the kind of thing that you would buy – the local blacksmith would make it in a friendly manner. No, it would not be suitable for a pitch fork, nor yet as a graip. It has lain in a barn for a long time and those who put it there no doubt knew how to use it.'

On the opposite side of the river, the road cuts across a strip of level land that was the traditional shinty pitch. It is said to have reached from the island of Morile to opposite Soilshan, roughly about a mile. The game of shinty is an interesting survival. It much resembles the Irish game of hurley that was played in very ancient times. The story of Cuchulain, the great hero of the Ulster epic, tells of an episode when, as a little boy, he was knocking along a ball with a hurley stick as he walked. Shinty is played with a 'puck' and not a ball, but how often does one see a school-boy 'dribbling' along a football as he goes. The incident illustrates the human, down-to-earthness of the old tales, so different to the idea of ethereal gloom initiated by Macpherson in Ossian. Shinty, as it was played in the late eighteenth century, was a formidable game. Sir Aeneas writes: 'The players' legs being frequently broke, may give it the name

Man Spearing Salmon with Leister. By Thomas Duncan, National Gallery of
Scotland.

of "Shiney".' He says it was sometimes played by one parish against another and that the players often came to blows. The winners got a share of a barrel of whisky and both sides became drunk.[7] I understand that the number of players was not limited and that all the available men and boys of both sides took part. According to a well-known local tale, a match always took place on New Year's Day by teams from Strath Nairn against Strathdearn (according to another version, the game was between the parishes of Moy and Dalarossie). One New Year's Day happened to fall on a Sunday, but, in spite of admonitions from the pulpit, the match was still played. Condemnation followed, and it is said that not only did all the players die young, but ever after, on a New Year's night, their spirits returned to replay the game. Considering the place to which the minister had consigned them, this might be regarded as a pleasant relaxation, but unfortunately no one that I ever met actually witnessed this spectral game. There seems to be a curious fashion in ghost stories for there is a tale that, on the night of the Battle of Culloden, the spirits of the dead of the opposing armies return each year to fight it again. This is *not* a local story.

There is a tradition that shinty was also played in a field beside Dalarossie church. Otherwise there are no records of local recreations. Sir Aeneas says that wrestling was popular and that school boys played ball with an inflated bladder.

During the Christmas Holy Days the country people, with hounds and terriers and armed with guns, poles, hooks, and spades, went fox hunting. When the fox went to ground, the terrier was sent down into his earth or he was dragged out by means of a hook fixed to the end of a pole. His tail was cut off and carried in triumph to the Chief's house where 'plenty of good cheer was ready'.[8]

The country people fished and also shot, mainly for the pot. There were Forestry Laws in Scotland as in England, but they were not rigorously enforced in the Highlands although there are cases of prosecutions, probably under provocation. In 1671 Alexander Mackintosh of Farr, who had also got into trouble for a 'ploy' on the Sabbath in Dalarossie church, was summoned at the High Court by Mackintosh for shooting deer in his Forest of Schephin (the old name for the land up the Strath). The revolutionary shift in the relative value of agricultural land and grouse moor was to be a phenomenon of the nineteenth and twentieth centuries.

Highlights in the people's lives were weddings and funerals. Sir Aeneas

Mackintosh described the procedure at a country wedding, and added that he and a party from Moy Hall often attended the dancing.[9] His generalized account is very similar to a more racy narrative for which I am indebted to Mr George Dixon who copied out for me an extract from a journal giving a delightful account by a Mr James Robertson of a wedding at Dalarossie in 1771. He was in Badenoch in the course of one of his expeditions to the Highlands on botanical research. He set out from Pitmain (on the outskirts of Kingussie) on 26 June and, having planned his route by map and compass, started to cross the mountains to the upper part of Strathdearn which, though ten miles distant, was the nearest inhabited place. He found snow still lying in some places and was overtaken by a hailstorm but, when he arrived much fatigued and soaking wet, the cottagers received him kindly and gave him goat's milk and bread, the only fare these cottagers afforded. This was but one instance of the wonderful hospitality that he wrote he had always received among the Highlanders, who would literally share their last morsel of bread with a stranger.

Hearing that there was to be a wedding and that the people were gathering in a nearby cottage for the ceremony of washing the bride's feet, he resolved to join the party and was welcomed and placed in the best seat where there was least smoke because the fire was in the middle of the floor. The house was lighted by splinters of resinous wood which sometimes gave a light 'better in power' than that of a candle. They were burned on 'a pillar' of stone almost three feet high beside the fire. He added that when the fireplace was at the end of the house the splinters were placed on a stone ledge behind it. He gave everyone snuff which the Highlanders never refuse and called for a bottle of *usque baugh* (whisky).

The bride 'was a buxon blithe widow of thirty' and she wore a special cap, very large with two long streamers hanging down her back. A fiddle was produced and the dancing, 'preceded by repeated bumpers of the *usque baugh*', went on till six o'clock in the morning. The party then sat down to a breakfast consisting of bowels of sheep mixed together and swimming in fat. After that followed curds and cream, then cheese and, last of all, *usque baugh*.

About half-past seven, the party set out for the church. The bride wore a tartan gown, a linen apron, a linen neckerchief, the large cap already mentioned and a tartan plaid and went out first with her maid on her right side and her bridegroom's man on the left. The bridegroom

Highland Wedding. By D. Allan, National Gallery of Scotland.

followed wearing a short coat, tartan kilt and hose and brogues. He also put a sixpence under his heel in his shoe before the nine-mile walk to church in order to defend him from witches. Before he set out, the bridegroom asked the bride's father if he were willing to let him marry his daughter, to which the father replied, 'Take her and God's blessing go with her.' As the company went towards the church, a gun was fired, as a salute, as they passed each group of houses. The ceremony was like that in all Presbyterian churches.

After the service the company, having refreshed themselves in a public house, returned home, but about eight o'clock that night the wedding party went to a barn where the mother of the bride had arranged a number of benches, the middle one with a cloth on it to serve as a table. Every man led in a woman, the bridegroom conducting the bride. As she entered her mother threw pieces of bread and cheese over her head — these pieces the attendants collected and ate. Supper consisted of boiled mutton and broth made with no vegetables; some oatmeal and a large piece of butter was put into each pot before serving so that the surface of the broth was covered as with oil. Before and after supper every guest had a bumper of *usque baugh*. This entertainment was provided by the newly married couple but, afterwards, the company paid for the liquor that they consumed, in some cases two bottles of whisky a head. Immediately after supper, the company began to dance. The bride and bridegroom, the bridesmaid and the bridesman led off the dancing. The dance lasted till two o'clock in the morning when everyone went home. There was no special ceremony over the bedding of the newly-wed couple.[10]

On the twenty-eighth the intrepid traveller set forth again. It is little wonder that, as Sir Aeneas points out, the cost of their wedding was a heavy burden and sometimes ruined a young couple. Even in the 1830s the custom persisted of a wedding feast provided by the hosts while the guests paid for what they afterwards drank.[11]

In the description of the wedding, Robertson mentions the wearing of Highland dress and, considering that it had been proscribed by law after the '45, this may sound surprising. There is, however, no evidence that the Act was enforced in Strathdearn and the wearing of Highland dress was only going out in the parish in the 1820s. I think the change is very significant. The growing volume of traffic on the road through Strathdearn was integrating what had been a secluded area with the rest of the country. The people were becoming merged into a far larger community but were losing their individual identity. The change was far deeper than the abandonment of a peculiar form of dress.

The *New Statistical Account* states that the most popular dyes were black, red, blue and green.[12] Red, blue and green are the colours that are combined in various proportions in the setts of the Mackintosh, Macgillivray and Macbean tartans, the clans to which most of the local people claimed relationship. The materials for dyeing red can be obtained locally, but to get a good red is a troublesome and difficult process as I know from many failures. I have never met a dyer who knew of local plants that would give either a blue or a green. Woad does not seem to grow in the North. In the West, where there is still a tradition of home-dyeing, I was told that indigo was used for blue and mixed with locally grown dye-stuffs for green. Most plants will give a muddy yellow and a skilled dyer can produce a brilliant and most lovely shade. What happened before indigo was available, I have never been able to discover. The significant fact is that, desperately poor as the country people were, they had sufficient personal and family pride to wear clothes of such exacting colours.

The other great social occasion in the people's lives was a funeral. According to Sir Aeneas the body was laid out and friends and relatives gathered to watch it during the night. A special air, known as a 'late wake' (the English lyke wake), was sung, then a good fire was made up. There was plenty of drink and snuff. The young folks played at 'country games' and the old ones told tales of ghosts and hobgoblins. The custom of dancing at the wake had been given up.[13] By the 1830s funerals were shorn of their conviviality and the mourners were limited by order of the Justices of the Peace to three glasses of drink each.[14]

One of the most marked characteristics of the people was their wonderful hospitality. James Robertson who was widely travelled in the Highlands wrote that the way he was received at the Coigs prompted him to pay

> a grateful tribute to the hospitality of the Highlanders, a quality in which they are outdone by no people on earth. They receive a stranger with a cheerful air, entertain him in the best manner they can, and devote themselves entirely to please him. During five summers I have travelled among them I was never once used unkindly − on the

contrary, I have oftener than once received a portion of the last morsel
of bread, even when my entertainer was ignorant of how he could obtain
any new supply.[15]

Harvest was the occasion for some festivity. The final sheaf was formally
laid up and, on the larger farms, there was the harvest feast. Reaping the
corn and most of the rest of the work was done communally and, until
the machine for clipping sheep and the baler for harvesting and hay-
making came into wide use, people came to help each other and were
entertained.

With the greater interest in religion that grew up in the eighteenth
century, the yearly Sacrament Sundays became important occasions in
the social life of the parish. People from surrounding parishes travelled
long distances to enjoy (they did!) the sermons by noted preachers and
the meetings on the preceding Friday 'for discussing religious topics' in
which members of the congregation sometimes took part. In the 1830s
congregations of 5000 people were usual.[16] Before the days of motor cars
there was much decorous hospitality given to the visitors and, even in my
young days, I remember that at one of these occasions there was not an
egg to be bought at the shop.

One likes to picture these houses in which all this happened. Even by
the 1830s the old local type of cottage was being replaced by conventional mason-built houses.[17] But, even more than a hundred years
later, a few cottages built in the traditional local style survived at the
Coigs.

In the Highlands several styles of buildings evolved to meet the special
needs and resources of the individual district. For instance, in the island of
Lewis, where there was no growing timber and very high winds, the
cottages were built with the minimum of wood and they were shaped so
as to offer the least possible resistance to the wind.

In the Eastern Highlands the main feature in the construction of the
houses was that of the 'couples', pairs of long pieces of timber, almost
invariably small tree-trunks — the 'cabers' that are now tossed at
Highland Games. The low dry-stone walls of the house were built round
the lower ends of each pair of couples and their top ends were crossed and
fastened together so that they formed an inverted 'V'. There might be
four of these couples in a cottage. A fifteenth-century poem by
Fionnlagh Ruadh, in praise of a MacGregor chief, describes a feast in such
a house.[18] The roof tree was laid along the crossed tops of the couples,

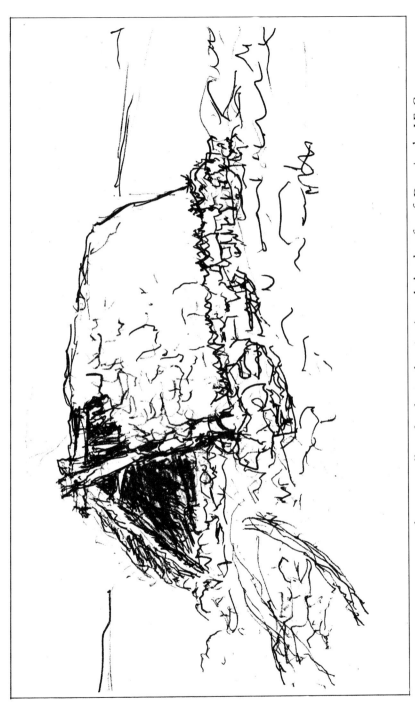

Ruined Cottage at Eile, upper valley of Dulnain, showing 'couples' and turf roof. Drawing by I.F. Grant.

hence the Gaelic toast, 'To your roof tree', and the junction of the couples was reinforced by a cross piece placed very high up. Over the couples and roof tree there was a framework of lighter pieces of wood pegged together with wooden pins, and over that a thick covering of sods of peat, each with one tapered end. These sods were arranged to overlap each other rather like a bird's feathers or the scales of a fish and the ends of the bundles of straw (or more rarely heather) used for the thatch were pushed under the edges of the overlapping sods. A fringe of heather along the edge of the roof carried off the drips. Originally, no doubt, the hearths in such houses were placed in the middle of the house and the smoke made its way out through a hole in the roof. But long before my day partition walls had been built with 'hanging chimneys' against them. A 'hanging chimney' was a long wooden structure, the top of which was narrowed to form the chimney and the lower end widened to form a canopy above the fire. From an iron bar across the chimney one or more iron chains hung down with hooks on which pots could be hung. I greatly deprecate the misuse of the term 'cruck', by people who study what they term 'vernacular' buildings, instead of 'couples', in referring to our very individual indigenous style of building. My nephew asked someone well versed in local ways of building if he knew what cruck meant. After some hesitation, he suggested that it might refer to a vessel for holding butter, thinking that my nephew meant 'crock'.

Two old tales that, for their point, depend upon the form of the old houses, have survived. One was told me in Strath Spey. Some fugitives from justice – perhaps Jacobites – took refuge in a cottage. Their pursuers were close on their heels and the only place to hide was between the couples and the roof. The pursuers, in the mirk of the cottage, did not see the hunted men, but their dogs smelled them out. The other story relates to Strath Nairn. Clan Mackintosh had become involved in a fierce quarrel with the Earl of Moray. The ins and outs of it are too complicated to tell here, but their Chief had died, his heir was a child and was in Moray's hands and the clansmen had chosen a captain to lead them. He was a man of outstanding ability, a kinsman of the Chief and his name was Hector. In reprisal for two ferocious raids, Moray gathered his feudal retainers to attack the Mackintoshes. He captured a number of them but Hector was able to escape. Moray held a court in a barn at Tordarroch in Strath Nairn and, one after another, eighteen men were questioned about the hiding place of Hector and, having refused to tell, were summarily hanged from the cross-piece of one of the couples.[19]

In the thirties when I was collecting exhibits for an exhibition of old Highland life it was a great privilege to visit one or two of these old cottages that had survived at the Coigs. I specially remember the welcome I used to get at Mrs Beaton's house and how beautiful she had made it. The rag rugs and the curtains of the box bed were all of subtle shades of faded red harmonizing with the glowing peat fire and contrasting with the warm darkness of the roof. But early travellers disapproved of such houses, notably Burt. A description of two of them he had to visit when he crossed the Findhorn on his way to Strath Spey are far from complimentary. They must indeed have been unhygienic, cramped and dark quarters for a whole family, especially in winter, when so much time had to be spent indoors. It was the genius of the people that made them the setting for the songs, stories, the proud traditions that their descendants nostalgically try to recall.

4

The Holding and Use of Land

Agriculture

After crossing the river, Mitchell's road mounts by easy gradients to a projecting elbow of the higher ground and, as one follows it, one can trace the long sequence of farms that border the river upon either side for some miles up the Strath. In 1793 the country was described as 'bleak and barren, rugged and mountainous, except small stripes and spots on each side of the River Findhorn'.[1] One can try to build up a mental picture of how the great changes in the layout of the land came about, of the social life of the people and of the alteration in the relative value of different kinds of land.

In Strathdearn the forest had first of all to be cleared. I have read that the nibbling of goats and sheep, especially the former, was one of the principal causes of the disappearance of Highland forests and woodlands. Being well acquainted with the ways of one Strathdearn goat, I can believe it. In the old days it was quite usual for Highlanders to keep goats. In some districts one or two of these escaped to the hills and established feral herds. Those of Strath Nairn were white. The goats on the Monadh Liath, near the Slochd, are grey, often with brown stripes down their cheeks; the billies sometimes carry very fine horns. Sir Aeneas Mackintosh noticed these goats. Bishop Forbes, in 1770, also noticed several goats on the steepest part of the Slochd, apparently 'hanging on by their beards and their feet'. Perhaps it is too much to hope that the present goats are descended from the ones that helped to clear the forest because hard winters on the bleak hill-tops kill off numbers of them, and there are occasional escapes by some of the few goats still kept in the district. According to a local tale the Strathdearn goats had their own use. When one sees goats and sheep feeding on the same hill face it is noticeable that the greenest patches tend to be occupied by the goats.

A local flock-master, wishing to protect the pasturage of his sheep, once tried to get rid of the goats. Thereupon some of the sheep went onto the rock face of the Slochd where there are enticing patches of tender grass in the sheltered crannies which had been the preserve of the goats. The sheep became stuck and the Fire Brigade from Inverness had to be sent for to rescue them. The goats thereafter were allowed to return to Slochd Muic.

The ways of farming that became firmly established in Strathdearn and lasted till less than two hundred years ago were very different to those of the present day. Farming was done by groups of people, generally by a tenant with a long lease – a tacksman – or by the holder of a feu (as was almost invariably the case in Strathdearn) and a number of sub-tenants. Less often it was carried on by a group of joint tenants. The names of a few farms in Strathdearn appear in sixteenth-century documents.

The appearance of the farms was quite different for neither hay, followed by a fallow, nor turnips was grown. The only crops were cereals – oats of an inferior kind, barley, bere (an inferior kind of barley) and rye. There were no rectangular fenced fields. On the best land (termed infield) these cereal crops were continuously grown and all the available manure was spread on the land. Patches of less fertile land (termed outfield) were cropped for a few years until the fertility of the soil was exhausted, and were then left to recover themselves while fresh pieces of land were ploughed up. As there were no fences the crops had to be protected from the animals by constant herding.

The land under cultivation was ploughed in long 'rigs', built higher and higher by successive ploughings. On an abandoned township at Glenkirk at the lower end of the Strath one can see, under the heather, the rigs of the old cultivation.

The rigs belonging to each of the joint cultivators were scattered and not held in one block. In a contemporary description the farms were said to be 'all inter woven'. There were two good reasons for this. In the first place, as the work had to be done by a number of the tenants working together, this ensured that everyone's land received equal attention. In the second place, as there was no control of the land by drainage, liming or fertilizers, it varied in quality and, as the joint tenants were subsistence farmers, dependent on what they grew for their actual food, it was important that, be the season dry or wet, each one got something off his land.

The implements were as primitive as the methods of farming. They ensured the maximum of effort for the smallest result. Iron was a luxury

Strathdearn Goat with slopes above Pollochaig in background.
Photograph by Mrs Rose.

and implements were mainly home-made of wood. For instance, the plough was crudely made of several pieces of wood, pinned together by wooden pins. Only the sock and the coulter were of iron and the construction was so simple that it could not turn a furrow but only make a shallow rut; sometimes the rig required more than one ploughing or the turf had to be cut by the preliminary use of an implement called a ristle.

The plough team on light Highland soil consisted of four of the little Highland horses, yoked abreast; three men were required to work the plough: one, walking backwards, to lead the horses, one to hold the stilts of the plough and one to give general help. Ploughing had to be done in great haste when the winter, prolonged in this high-lying Strath, gave place to a brief time in which it was necessary to prepare the ground and to sow it.

In the summer a large number of people and livestock used to go up to the shielings where the cattle throve on the sweet hill pasture. From the milch cattle a supply of cheeses was made for winter consumption and the beef cattle were fattened for sale at the autumn 'trysts' (cattle sales). But at home there was also work to do, for the peats had to be cut, dried and carried home for the year's fuel.

In the autumn there was often a long agonizing wait as the corn slowly ripened, winter inexorably approached and day and night the animals had to be herded and folded to keep them out of the corn. Harvesting was done by groups of reapers using the sickle and then binding and stooking the sheaves.

Often the corn had to be cut before it had properly ripened and dried. The latter process had to be finished in kilns over a peat fire. Every farm seemed to have one of these small kilns — a low stone wall enclosing a peat fire over which a framework of branches was arranged to support the corn. During the long, long winter the men threshed the corn and the women spun the wool.

The return for so much labour by so many people was meagre. According to the *Old Statistical Account* 'in favourable years the produce is nearly equal to the consumption of the parish'.[2] Even in the more fertile land of Strath Spey the produce of the farms was barely adequate.[3] The people were dependent on their livestock for dairy products to supplement their diet and on animals to sell to earn all the money they had.[4]

The livestock kept upon the farm in the old days were also different to those on a modern farm. Each farmer kept several of the small Highland horses – Burt called them 'miniatures'. The farmer had to contribute a beast to the common plough-team and all transport had to be done by pack or pannier – corn to the mill, peats from the moss, paraphernalia to and from the shielings, etc.

The number of sheep kept by each farmer was small. They were kept for their milk, especially to make cheese, and their wool for spinning at home. They were small delicate beasts with fine fleeces – they had to be housed during the winter and pastured about the farm in the summer. One of the great changes in local farming came about with the introduction of the hardy, coarse-woolled, black-faced sheep. These spent the summer on the moors which, in the old days, were entirely unproductive, and were wintered on the lower ground.

In the old days the raising of cattle was infinitely more important and more esteemed than the raising of sheep. The ill-fed cows only calved every second year and so, to supply a family with the cheese, butter and milk on which they so much depended, at least two milch cows had to be kept. Their 'followers', calves and stirks, were the farmer's sole source of money for rent, other dues, grain in times of shortage and general expenses.

During the summer almost the entire stock was sent up to the shielings, areas of natural grass at the head waters of rivers or burns. There they did well and recovered from the privations of the rest of the year; the young cattle reached their most saleable condition before the autumn market. During autumn, winter and spring most of the animals existed on what they could pick up of natural grass and the stubble on the fields. The animals that had to be housed during the winter were fed on straw. The mortality among the livestock must have been very high, but I have only once seen it estimated in figures and it was put at one in five of the cattle every winter. Burt, whose sympathy with the 'little horses' rather redeems his patronizing attitude to the Highlanders, gives a moving account of the struggles of the poor, little, underfed beasts to work. The other animals must have been in an equally miserable condition and, in springtime the cows that had been housed had to be lifted out to the grass.

A present-day farmer in Strathdearn, if he kept cattle, would have to house them for at least five months of the year and the costs of feeding and labour would be exceedingly high.[5] Milk is entirely supplied from a dairy near Inverness nowadays.

Such were the conditions of the lesser joint farmers during most years, with some considerable seasonal variations; but at irregular intervals which, in more exposed districts such as Strathdearn, might average less than ten years, there was a serious dearth when people resorted to such desperate expedients as consuming the corn set aside for sowing next year's crops or of bleeding the milch cattle. The dates of specially terrible dearths were in the 'Year of the Sidd' (1602),[6] the Ill Years of King William, the 'Year of the White Pease' (1782) and the Years of the Short Crops, 1814-16 and 1826.[7]

There are two stories about local dearths. For the first I am indebted to Mr Murdo MacAskill. In a terrible dearth in Strathdearn there was 'hardly a smoke to be seen' anywhere (i.e. hardly an inhabited house) because all the people had gone to the low country to beg for food. At a mill that once stood at Casdae some people were found lying dead after licking the mill-stone. The mill disappeared long ago. It was, apparently, at a place near Dalmagarry where Wade's road and the later road are close together and the ground has been much disturbed. Old meal mills were sometimes very small, their mill-wheels less than six feet high and therefore needing little water power.

I heard the other story as a child. Looking up the Strath a little white house was pointed out to me. I was told that it was built on the site of an older house and that, in a dearth, the farmer who lived there had managed to save a little corn. Late one night, and desperate for food for their families, two of his neighbours planned to take his corn by force, but a third man said it was shameful to rob a neighbour however great their own need. They argued all night and, at last, in the grey before the dawn, the two were won over and gave up their plan.

We have an official report on a terrible famine that occurred in 1783. Even the more fertile districts suffered. In the evidence submitted it was reported from Inverness that there were 'many good farmers with their wives and children begging in the streets. Last harvest has finished most of them. Meal or any kind of victuals cannot be had for love or money. Before the winter is over people will die in the streets.' A Badenoch factor reported that he had given a man £80 to try to buy meal to keep his tenants alive till the next potato crop. The man went through Strath Spey, Strathavon, Glenlivet, Inveravon, Knockando and over to Elgin, but failed to get any meal. James Grant stated that there were grounds for apprehending that the spirit of emigration which, to his certain knowledge 'is very high, may become general'.[8]

Such were the traditions of dire want that shocked Edmund Burt although he was used to the conditions of rural living in England in the early eighteenth century, which were themselves pretty low.

The Forest

The change from forest to these patches of farmland must have been a slow one. For a long time the land was mainly used for hunting and for summer pasturage. Even so late as 1793 the land was let in 'lumps' or pieces and not in acres because it was mainly used for pasturage and not tillage.[9] In the twelfth century, when written records first bring the district within our definite ken, the Bishop of Moray was made the Superior of Strathdearn and of the upper part of Strath Spey and, as we have seen, the parishes of Moy and Dalarossie were formally constituted as part of the general process of organizing medieval Scotland. They were both served by one priest. In 1163 Malcolm IV finally ended a series of revolts led by members of a rival branch of the royal line and 'planted' the province with his loyal supporters. Among them was Shaw, a younger son of Earl = Thane = *Toiseach* of Fife = Mackintosh. He got a grant of Petty, a small area (about eight square miles) of very fertile land in the Laich of Moray, and also of the Forest of Strathdearn. The terms of the first grant were indefinite but a descendant of Shaw, the first Mackintosh, got a lease of the Barony of Moy from the Bishop of Moray in 1336 and, after the War of Independence, the King granted the greater part of Strathdearn to the Earl of Moray. After the Reformation the Earl of Huntly obtained the very top of it.

The Mackintoshes evidently used their land in Strathdearn for pasturage and for hunting. One of them, Lachlan (14th Chief), was murdered there in 1524 while hunting. In one time of great peril the Chiefs of Mackintosh used the land as a refuge but, as they managed to get leases for more land in the Laich of Moray, in Strath Spey and even in Lochaber, for centuries they did not live permanently in Strathdearn.

Other people enjoyed the pleasures of hunting in Strathdearn. Sir Aeneas in his *Notes* writes:

Countrys \that are coverd with wood (as Scotland was) harboured numbers of wild beasts, and as hunting much resembles War the Gentlemen of Scotland gave much of their time to it, for attending very little to Agriculture they were always happy to be employed in the favourite pursuit; consequently when they formed hunting partys it had more the appearance of going against a powerfull Enemy than against the timid Deer or Voratious Wolf. No Dogs were used, and the method followed was this, — When any Chief chose to hunt, he fixes a day, and Acquaints the neighbouring Chiefs and his own Clan of his Intention, who are to appear Armed at the place appointed. People called *Trickhell* men go round the Country the day before to find the Haunts of the Deer, which when discovered is the place of Rendezvous.[10]

There are many descriptions of such hunts, some of which were of historical importance, such as that at which the Earl of Mar plotted the Rising of the '15. Unfortunately there is no tradition of the scene of such a hunt in Strathdearn nor does the word *elrig* (the term for where the driven deer were actually killed), which has become a place-name in several districts, occur in Strathdearn. The actual slaughter was followed by an open-air feast, fires were lighted and some of the venison roasted — in fact it was an ancient Highland version of the barbecue.

We rather pride ourselves that, in our modern sophistication, we have acquired an appreciation of natural surroundings. But not only did Calder (afterwards Campbell) of Cawdor and Rose of Kilravock, rich landowners in the fertile Laich of Moray, acquire land in Strathdearn, but in 1409 Ferquhard (9th Chief of Mackintosh), 'being of an indolent, melancholy and reserved nature' and being 'wholly given up to ease', resigned for himself and his children his portion and inheritance as Chief, only retaining Kyllachie and Corrivory. Kyllachie is a long stretch of farmland, woods and hillside extending up the valley from about the point where Mitchell's bridge crossed the river.

Then, with the beginning of the seventeenth century, new factors came into play bringing great changes in the life of the Strath.

The Coming of the Farming Lairds

A change in the economic development of Scotland in the seventeenth century had a special effect on the whole of the Highlands and, therefore, on Strathdearn. After the Union of the Crowns the cattle-droving trade with England became more and more important. Ever-increasing numbers of cattle were raised in the Highlands and Islands, collected into droves in the autumn when they were in good condition after summer pasturage at the shielings, sold at the various trysts, and driven for winter feeding down to England. The local tryst, at least by the eighteenth century, was at Dalmagarry. The next and larger gathering place was at Pitmain (on the outskirts of the more modern village of Kingussie). Pitmain was on one of the great drove routes from the Northern Highlands and over the hill passes to the final tryst at Falkirk. From there the cattle were driven to England.

As the demand for cattle increased, so did the need for summer pasturage, which was especially important for getting the saleable beasts into condition. The late Dr Victor Gaffney made an exhaustive study of shielings, especially those of the Cairngorms.[11] He kindly showed me his wonderful collection of photographs of shielings and photostats of the urgent letters of the tacksman of Strath Spey, among them my forebears on the Grant side, trying to get more shielings and of the straits that they were put to if they lost them.

It must have been due to this pressing need that the greater part of Strathdearn – the right bank of the Findhorn down to the defile of the Streens and both banks from a point between Freeburn and Dalmagarry up to a point further up the Strath than one can see from the road – was feued to eight individuals during the first half of the seventeenth century. The rest of the Strath – the lowest part of the left bank down to the Streens and the head waters of the Strath were held by Mackintosh of Mackintosh. Down to the present day these estates (all but one) have retained their identity although, in most cases, their ownership has changed. They are Kyllachie, 1616; Dalmigavie, 1614; Aberarder, 1634; Corriebrough Beg, very early; Holm, 1620; Corriebrough Mor (now Balnespick), 1632; Clune, early; and Tomatin 1639. All of these are feued from the Earl of Moray with the exception of Dalmigavie which was feued from Calder (now Campbell) of Cawdor.

Six of the new owners were Mackintoshes and the other two, Macbean of Tomatin and MacQueen of Corriebrough Beg, belonged to clans that are very closely associated with the Mackintoshes and are members of Clan Chattan (the association of clans of which Mackintosh of Mackintosh is recognized Chief). The ancestor of Macbean, who got a feu of Tomatin, had been the earliest adherent of the Mackintoshes in the thirteenth century and had supported the emerging clan in its fight for survival against the Comyns. Members of the MacQueen family had come to Strathdearn in the fifteenth century in attendance upon Mora, daughter of Clan Ranald of Moidart, when she married Malcolm, 10th Chief of Mackintosh. A descendant got a feu of Corriebrough Beg.[12]

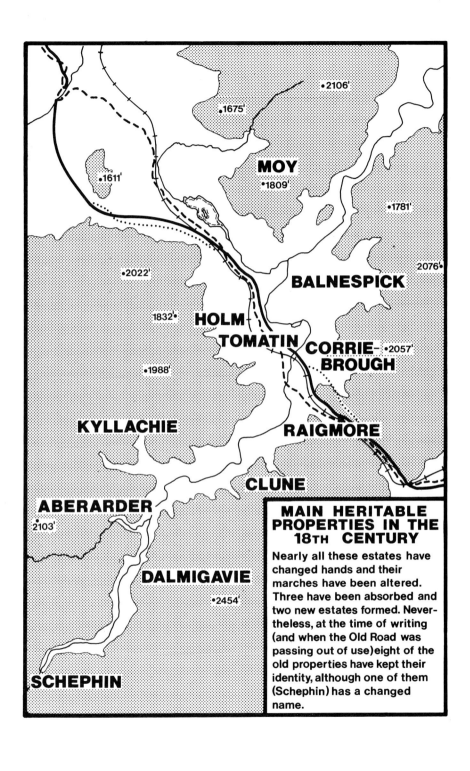

MOY

•2106'

•1675'

•1611'

•1809'

•1781'

•2022'

2076•

BALNESPICK

1832•

HOLM

TOMATIN

CORRIE-
BROUGH

•2057'

•1988'

KYLLACHIE

RAIGMORE

CLUNE

ABERARDER

2103'

DALMIGAVIE

•2454'

SCHEPHIN

**MAIN HERITABLE
PROPERTIES IN THE
18TH CENTURY**

Nearly all these estates have
changed hands and their
marches have been altered.
Three have been absorbed and
two new estates formed. Nevertheless, at the time of writing
(and when the Old Road was
passing out of use) eight of the
old properties have kept their
identity, although one of them
(Schephin) has a changed
name.

Of the remaining feu holders, five were the grandsons or great-grandsons of Chiefs of Mackintosh. Their families had been provided for by leases or as 'kindly tenants' of small pieces of the family estates in the Laich of Moray. They had prospered sufficiently to acquire one or more small pieces of land scattered about the district and so had made enough money to obtain a feu of a large bit of cattle-raising land in Strathdearn from the Earl of Moray. In the case of all but two it would appear that the arrangement was an ordinary transaction. But in the case of two, Mackintosh of Kyllachie and Mackintosh of Corriebrough Mor, it was very different.

The Mackintoshes of Kyllachie were descended from Alan, a younger son of the 10th Chief. His family occupied land in Petty, were active in clan affairs, added to their possessions and, in 1614, Lachlan, his great-great-grandson, got a feu of Dalmigavie from Cawdor, apparently an ordinary transaction.

Unfortunately for the Mackintoshes the Earls of Moray and Huntly, the two nobles who held the superiorities of the scattered lands that they occupied, had struck up a sudden friendship – generally they were bitter rivals. Mackintosh and some of his clansmen had lived on the fertile coastal lands of Petty since the thirteenth century as Moray's 'kindly tenants' and had been his loyal supporters. But in 1622, under the influence of Huntly, Moray, in order to obtain higher rents, ordered all his tenants in Petty, the majority of whom were Mackintoshes, to remove themselves. They obeyed and it was obviously in preparation for this that Moray, in 1616, gave Lachlan Mackintosh a feu of Kyllachie for a yearly rent of forty merks, 'a mart, a sheep and a kid yearly', upon condition that he removed from Petty.[13]

The matter was not, however, allowed to rest. At the time of the evictions the Chief, who was obviously a very sick man for he died soon afterwards, submitted to Moray's legal rights and did nothing. But after his death his heir was still only a child who could not fulfil his duties and defend his clansmen, and his 'tutor' (old term for guardian) did not do it for him, so members of the clan took the matter into their own hands. In 1624 two hundred of them, under the leadership of Lachlan, uncle of the young Chief and Lachlan, son of Mackintosh of Kyllachie, gathered to exact vengeance.

In the words of John Spalding in the *History of the Troubles and Memorable Transactions in Scotland and England from MDCXXIV to MDCXLV*, after vainly craving from the Earl their kindly possessions, they resolved to recover the land by force of arms or 'to cast the samen waist, and none should labour the ground or pay any duetie to the earle'.

Accordingly they 'brake out in arms' and 'keeped the feilds in their highland weid upon foot, with swords, bowes, arrowes, targes, hagbuttis, pistolls, and other highland armour; and first begane to rob and spouilzie the earle's tennents who laboured their possessions, of their haill goods, geir, insight plenishing, horse, nolt, sheep, corns and cattell'. They then went 'sorning' through Moray and as far beyond as Glen Urquhart and perhaps further, 'takeing their meat and food per force wher they could not gett it willingly, frae freinds alseweill as frae their faes; yet still keeped themselves from shedeing of innocent blood'. And they declared that they had 'tane this course to gett their own possessions again, or then hold the country walking'.[14]

Moray raised a force, mainly of Macgregors from his Menteith property, and sent out parties to try to catch the raiders but was unsuccessful. Possibly the Macgregors had too much fellow feeling for the delinquents and avoided catching them. Finally Moray obtained the office of Lieutenant in the North in order to have power to declare the leaders who, besides the Mackintoshes included MacQueen of Corriebrough Beg, to be rebels; he was able to issue Letters of Intercommuning forbidding all persons under severe penalties to give them shelter or help. This deprived the outlaws of a great deal of support and made it impossible for them to continue their defiance for long.

Fortunately for them Moray's appointment as Lieutenant of the North annoyed Huntly (who had incited him to get rid of his faithful old tenants from Petty) and the two Earls quarrelled and Moray, dependant as he was on Clan Mackintosh as a formidable element among his supporters, made peace with the outlaws. The land was restored to the tenants of Petty and the penalties against the outlaws were revoked upon condition that they do Moray's work as Lieutenant of the North and catch a notorious murderer and robber, James Grant of Carron. Moray also made a profit by collecting fines from people who had disobeyed the Letters of Intercommuning and befriended the Mackintosh outlaws.[15] This was the third time the Mackintoshes were ejected from Petty and regained possession of it by force. They had already done so in 1330, 1513, and now in 1622.

James Grant was the uncle of Grant of Carron. His family and that of Grant of Ballindalloch had been at feud for some time and all the enormities were not confined to one side. The Grants of Ballindalloch, however, were the first to get the ear of the Privy Council. James Grant was summoned to appear before the Earl of Moray for a series of outrages against the Ballindallochs. He fled the country, but then returned and became the leader of thirty or forty 'broken Highlanders and ane opin reaver, sorner and oppressioner'. Moray, as Lieutenant of the North, was responsible for catching him and 'resolves to gar one devill ding another'; to that effect agreed with Lachlan Mackintosh, the uncle of the Chief, William Mackintosh, son of Kyllachie, and a George Dallas to take the said James Grant whether dead or alive.

Accordingly the three men collected about forty strong clansmen well armed after the Highland fashion and a party of them traced James Grant to a house in Auchnachyll in Strathavan. He had with him ten men and his son. The Mackintoshes 'pursued the house most furiously; the said James and his men wins out and takes the flight, they follow sharply, slew four of his men, wounded himselfe with arrows in eleven sundrie parts of his body, and when he could doe no more, he was taken, and his other six men, but his bastard son wan away'.[16] James Grant was imprisoned but was able to make his escape.

Lachlan Mackintosh received a feu of Corriebrough Mor. The name of Lachlan's new possession was later changed in deference to the wishes of his descendants when they sold it in 1791. To prevent confusion, it is better to call it by its new name, Balnespick. It was bought by my mother's great-grandfather and he took the name of his grandfather's wadset in Rothiemurchus. The name has an old family tradition attached to it. When Rothiemurchus was all church land a Grant who was living there incurred the displeasure of the Bishop of Moray. The Bishop imprisoned him in his Castle of Spynie and the Laird of Grant, as his duty was, took up the cause of his clansman, but unfortunately the poor man died in prison. Grant, however, was able to make good his cause and held the land himself. It was ever after called Baile an Easbuig, i.e. Balnespick.

The tradition is interesting because it has a foundation of fact. There is a more circumstantial story that the Laird of Grant got the lands of Muckrach from the Bishop in compensation due to a Grant of Achernack and that he gave the lands to one of his sons. It is a fact that his son in 1575 received instead the lands of Rothiemurchus.[17] A wadset of Balnespick a holding in Rothiemurchus was given as the provision for a younger son to the ancestor of my mother's people.

For over one hundred years, till the great changes brought about after the '45, there seems to have been little alteration in the way of life of the group of feu holders in Strathdearn. They all maintained their hold on more fertile lands in the low country (Kyllachie was particularly successful in increasing his holdings of land). The source of their living continued to be from agriculture and one pictures them as organizing the feeding and wintering of stock during the winter on their low country land and its summering on the pastures of Strathdearn. Their incomes were probably small and fluctuated with the climate. The courtly manners and good breeding, the pride and the extreme poverty of the Highland gentlemen of this period were proverbial. Figures are not available, but an interesting example of the simplicity of their possessions exists. The text of the will of Lachlan Mackintosh of Kinrara in Badenoch, dated 1686, has been preserved. He was the uncle of the Chief and he probably had a rather better property than had any of the group in Strathdearn. He left the 'use' of his silver spoons, his brewing kettle and his mortar and pistole to his wife during her dwelling at Contullich and, thereafter, to his nephew. These are the only possessions apart from weapons mentioned. He left his nephew his sword, best gun and bow and arrows. Another nephew was to get a gun and a third a short gun and holster and pistol. He left some bonds to his son-in-law (not to his daughter!) because his wife was 'ane aged and tender woman' and he wished him and his daughter to 'repair' to the house he had left her to manage her affairs and 'keepe her as a persone of her quality in mantinence, apparell and money'.[18] Another illustration of the narrowness of their means is the collapse of the Mackintoshes of Strone and Gask. They were evidently people of good position. Several members were 'out' in the '15 and one of them was condemned to death. To obtain his release the family was involved in much expense and had to borrow 1000 merks Scots. This ruined them and it was lucky for William, a cadet of the family, that he had been provided for by the grant of the wadset of Balnespick.[19]

One gets some idea of the social standing of these farmer lairds by the marriages that they made. These, of course, were generally with members of families in their own position, but quite frequently with the younger sons (not the heirs) or the daughters of far more considerable land-owners. They took an active and leading part in the affairs of the clan but they lived within a very narrow world from which there was little chance of escape. The very limited amount of land and resources had to be divided or shared so as to provide for younger sons. The chance of faring forth to seek their fortune in the way so characteristic of the same families in the second half of the eighteenth century was only beginning to be grasped in Strath Spey, and it was well into the second half of the century before it became general in Strathdearn.

One has to remember that, all through the period, although they were carrying on the workaday life of farmers, they were living in, and taking an active part in, a state of civil war. Clan Mackintosh and its associates took a leading part in the Jacobite Risings of the '15 and the '45. There had been two long-standing feuds over the claims of the Chief to land in Lochaber. The feud with the Camerons went back to 1337 and in its early stages gave rise to the fight on the Inches at Perth between Clan Cai (Clan Chattan) and Clan Qwhewyl (the Camerons). It was settled in 1665 when £48,300 Scots was paid to Mackintosh in compensation. The feud with Macdonald of Keppoch had begun in the fifteenth century and ended in 1698. It was the costlier of the two for the people of Strathdearn. Mackintosh suffered a humiliating defeat at the Battle of Mulroy in which Kyllachie lost one son and Dalmigavie two and Keppoch took advantage of Dundee's Rising to make a devastating raid on Mackintosh lands. From the formal claim for restitution one gathers that he plundered the Mackintosh lands in upper Strath Spey, burning Dunachton, the Chief's house and also severely raiding Strath Nairn. From there Keppoch worked havoc on Mackintosh lands of Moy in Strathdearn and also, by a drove road over the hills, attacked Dalmigavie.[20]

Besides these long-standing feuds, the Strath itself was exposed to constant reiving from the west, and there was a saying that the people of Strathdearn used to eat their beef before their broth to make sure that it was not stolen from them. When I was young there was still a living tradition of what was probably the last of these sporadic raids. A small number of reivers attacked Balmore, a farm on Balnespick at the lower end of the Strath. The local people went to the assistance of the farmer, cutting off the raiders' retreat who ran up the hillside and were overtaken at a point beside the Bruach burn. There was a fight and one was killed. He was buried at a place higher up the burn. I know that I am not alone in experiencing a strange feeling that something had happened at that place.

Cattle were the prime source of food and of money in the Highlands and, especially after the Union of the Crowns, there was such an impetus to the trade in them that cattle raiding may be said to have become commercialized. There was an old saying that 'Highland lairds counted their daughters' tochers by the light of the Martinmas moon', in other words, in autumn, just before the cattle, now in good condition after their summer grazing in the hills, were driven to the trysts. This was the favourite time for the raids. Graham of Gartmore, writing shortly before the '45, put the value of the herds of animals being stolen (mainly cattle) at £5000 and, as they were valued at about £3 a head, one gets some idea of the numbers involved. He put the cost of 'black mail', or payment for protecting them, at £5000. The fertile coastal lands by the Moray Firth were, in the words of a letter from Lochiel to the Laird of Grant, apologizing because the cattle of one of his clansmen had been raided by mistake: 'Moray land where all men taken their prey.' Cattle were the main objective of the hungry clansmen from Lochaber, the Rough Bounds and Glen Coe – cattle reiving was said to be Keppoch's main source of income. The raiders' favourite route was through the narrow defile, known as the Streens, where the Findhorn forces its way from Strathdearn to the low country and the sea. The raiders then drove their cattle up Strathdearn, over one of the easy passes to the valley of the Dulnain and on to Badenoch or northwards by way of Strath Errick to Lochaber.[21]

After passing Tomatin one can look down at the lower end of Strathdearn to the dark gash of the entrance to the Streens in the barrier of hills. On the top of the hill on the right there are the remains of a roughly built little watch-tower from which the local 'watch' kept a nightly lookout during the raiding season. Kyllachie was Captain of the Watch in Strathdearn and Cluny Macpherson in Badenoch. The lairds and farmers in Moray paid them and their men a regular contribution for keeping watch and stopping the raiders; a business-like receipt from Cluny to the Laird of Gordonstoun for his payment still exists.

In my youth, a story was still told of an exploit by Little John MacAndrew, a member of the Watch. He was a noted marksman with the crossbow which probably places him about the seventeenth century. He lived at Dalnahaitnich, in the valley of the Dulnain not far below the Slochd. In one raid Little John MacAndrew shot a raider; in another version he shot the whole of a raiding party, except one man who escaped. Kyllachie called out his congratulations and Little John cursed him roundly because he had named him and he knew that the escaping raider would carry back the information and that revenge was inevitable. The cattle raiders did indeed decide to kill him, and a party of them came to his house one winter's day. Little John was sitting by the fire when they came to the door. His quick-witted wife must have recognized their Lochaber accent for she turned on her husband, rating him as a presumptuous herd-boy daring to sit in his master's house by the fire. She drove him out of the house and welcomed the raiders as belated travellers and regretted that her husband was up the hill. She gave them food and a dram and, while they were thus engaged, she took Little John's crossbow from its place and slipped it through the window – Little John was lurking outside. He took the crossbow, climbed a tree that was near the house and picked off the raiders one by one as they left the house.

An important family that was settled in Strathdearn long before the group of lairds I have written about, was in rather the same social category. Right at the lower end, at the entrance to the Streens is Pollochaig. It lay just outside the barony of Moy and was held, it is claimed, for 300 years from the Earl of Moray by a branch of the MacQueen family, probably as a kindly tenant. In earlier times, MacQueen is said to have been a forester to the Earl. I was brought up on a tradition that a member of the family killed the last wolf in Scotland and I have heard variants of the tale that he shot a witch with a silver bullet, while she was in the form of a hare, wounding her and that she cursed him; thereafter the family fortunes failed and MacQueen had to give up Pollochaig.

There is, however, a stranger story collected by Fraser-Mackintosh from an older source. It is worth telling because it shows much vivid coherence of traditional fairy-lore compared with the fragments that were all that could be gathered even in my very young days. The wife of a kinsman of Macgillivray of Dunmaglass was stolen by the fairies and concealed in a fairy hill close by. To get into it, in order to rescue her, Macgillivray sent a messenger to MacQueen of Pollochaig to ask him for one of three candles of magic power that were known to be in his possession. MacQueen gave one of the candles but warned the messenger not to look backwards over his shoulder.

When the messenger, on his way back, reached a point close to Moy he heard a loud noise behind him, the trampling of horses, the shouting of men; he looked back and the candle was snatched from him.

A second messenger was sent. MacQueen gave him the second candle and he made his way back to Dunmaglass. But when he was about to cross the Nairn there was the same terrible noise and he looked back. The candle was snatched from him.

A third messenger was sent. MacQueen, with great generosity, gave him the third candle. The Findhorn was in spate* and he was afraid to cross it so he went back to MacQueen who gave him a stone to throw across the river. When he did so, he found himself on the other side and made his way back by a circuitous route without incident. Macgillivray's son took the candle, entered the fairy dun and rescued the woman. She would not believe she had been away a year and thought that she had only danced one reel. The fairies took their revenge. Shortly afterwards young Macgillivray's favourite horse turned on him and killed him.[22]

The Going of the Farming Lairds

The '45 and its aftermath is a milestone in Highland history. The face of the land, upon either side of our road, shows how completely the way of life of the Strath changed. Unfortunately it is easier to trace the progress of some of these changes than others.

It is mainly within the second half of the eighteenth century that the farming lairds changed from being dependent upon farming to following a profession or business outside – sometimes as far away as India or the New World. Every family had a member, sometimes several, serving in the Army. Sir James Mackintosh of Kyllachie held a high legal position in India, wrote several highly esteemed legal treatises and received the honour of a knighthood. Mackintosh of Aberarder also followed the law. The Macbeans of Tomatin were successful in business in Glasgow and London. One Mackintosh of Dalmigavie was a sea captain. One MacQueen of Corriebrough went into the Church and there was a strong connection with the Army. In my own family, one younger son was in the Army and served with distinction in the Peninsular War. Another emigrated to America. The heads of the family went on farming for two more generations. My grandfather had to retrieve the family fortunes by planting indigo in India. The Highland estates and larger farms were becoming places to retire to and enjoy. Sir Aeneas Mackintosh commented in the late eighteenth century that the local gentry preferred hunting to agriculture.

In *Memoirs of a Highland Lady* Miss Elizabeth Grant of Rothiemurchus gives a vivid picture of Highland society at the turn of that century. She describes the simplicity and good breeding, the survival of traditions of an older way of life by people who also had come into contact with the

---

* As a matter of fact he would not have to cross the Findhorn: the large Funtack burn was probably meant.

sophistication of 'the Age of Elegance', and many of whom had literally 'seen the world' when travelling was an adventure and the ways of life of different peoples and classes showed far more variety.

Sir Aeneas Mackintosh described the home of a close friend, Sheriff MacQueen of Corriebrough, as consisting 'only of a long stone and turf house having one floor, the office houses formed with the house two sides of a square'. In the steading of old farms one can find the remains of what was once the dwelling house, an advance on the houses built of 'couples' I described earlier, because the supporting timbers are built into solid masonry walls. Good examples have been noted in Strath Spey; the steading at Balmore (on Balnespick) is much of this type and Mr MacAskill, with a more intimate knowledge of the district, saw a few more examples before they were destroyed.

When they were in a position to build houses in the contemporary style they were unpretentious. Sir Aeneas described Dalmagarry Inn, built in 1732. It consisted of a two-storied building of four rooms and garrets. It supplied a bottle of excellent claret at 2/6 a bottle. Sir Aeneas also made a sketch of the new house built about 1700, as Mackintosh's principal residence, on the shores of Loch Moy. It was a perfectly plain building, in the Georgian style, of two storeys and a wing at the back, with no embellishments or provision for defences. It was totally unlike the 'tower houses' of the seventeenth century or the castellated mansions of the Victorian era.[23]

Brigadier Mackintosh, 'Old Borlum', who had travelled so widely in the Highlands as a Jacobite agent, writing in 1729, deplored the import of foreign goods to replace our own products:

> Where I once saw the Gentleman, Lady and Children dress'd clean and neat in home-spun stuffs, of her own sheeps growth and womens spinning, I see now the Ladys dress'd in French or Italian silks and brocades and the Laird and his sons in English broadcloth. Where I saw the table serv'd in Scots clean fine linen, I see now Fleemish and Dutch diaper and damask. And where, with two or three substantial dishes of beef, mutton and fowl, garnish'd with their own wholesome gravy, I see now served up several services of little expensive ashets with English pickles, yea Indian mangoes, and catch-up or anchovy sauces.

He regretted the change from 'the quaighful of good wholesome ale' and 'the dram of good wholesome Scots spirits' as a morning drink to the 'tea-kettle put to the fire, the tea-table and silver and china equipage brought in with the marmalet cream and cold tea'.[24]

In truth new contacts made old ways of living distasteful. Mr MacAskill wrote down for me the following sad story of the arrival in the North of 'the rather genteel young woman' from 'somewhere in the Low Country' that Captain MacQueen of Ards (the farm in front of Tomatin shop) had married. For some reason he had not brought her home with him and so at last she came up alone by coach and enquired for Captain MacQueen's residence at Tomatin; she found a low detached house built of dry stone and turf.

'Is this Captain MacQueen's house?' she asked of the old serving woman who came to the door.

'Yes.'

'I am Captain MacQueen's wife.'

'Oh, then you'd better come in.'

From a seat beside the fire she looked round the room and up at the smoke-blackened couples. 'What is Captain MacQueen doing?'

'He's up at the peat moss. He'll be home for his supper soon.'

'Where does Captain MacQueen sleep?'

She was led into a very dimly lit room.

'And where is Captain MacQueen's bed?'

The old woman pointed to some blankets laid over a bed of dry bracken. There the story ends.

Unfortunately the old revenues from the estates and farms were inadequate for the new standard of living. For instance, Sir James Mackintosh of Kyllachie, who had made his home in London, heavily burdened his estate and, as Holm and Aberarder through inter-marriages had become more or less merged with Kyllachie, in 1804 they were all sold to a kinsman, Mackintosh of Drummond, and then resold, a wonderful but, alas! transient renewal of old associations. A distant kinsman, William Mackintosh, after a brilliant career at the Bar, was raised to the Bench as Lord Kyllachie and bought the estate in 1881. Unfortunately, since then the place has had to be sold twice more. The new owners, in turn, have felt the special affection that this place always seems to have inspired.

The family of Mackintosh of Dalmigavie died out, the estate passed to a cousin and eventually, in 1897, was sold to Mr Mackenzie the owner of Farr (which had long passed from Mackintosh ownership).[25] Macbean of

Tomatin, with business interests in the South and overseas, continued to flourish. One sees evidence of the family's enterprise when the road passes through Tomatin. The place remained in Macbean hands until well within my memory and the family who have succeeded them are fully and actively identified with the life of the district. When so few people of this old name are in Strathdearn it is very pleasant that a devoted member of this clan – in spite of the fact that she has changed her name to Scarlett – has returned to the district.

From the middle of the eighteenth century the family of MacQueens of Corriebrough had followed the professions of the Church, the Army and the Law, but the estate had gradually got into increasing difficulties and was sold in 1817 to a developer, a Mr Campbell Smith, who felled the timber and cleared the people from all the eleven holdings on the estate. This, so far as I can ascertain, was the only instance of wholesale clearing in Strathdearn. Fortunately, the estate fell into very good hands. In 1844 it was bought by Mr Malkin.[26] His family, although their working life had to be spent elsewhere, not only beautified the place, but were on the friendliest terms with the people who worked for them on the farm and the estate. They were the first of the new incoming purchasers of land in Strathdearn to set a standard of identification with Strathdearn and its traditions. It was a source of pride to them and to the community that their managers, father and son, were descendants of the 'Captain of Five', a hero of a local episode in the '45. Once again the estate had to be sold and once more the new owners care for and love it.

During this period of change and the dissolution of old bonds, there was one new landowner with associations of especial interest. As I have tried to show, a group of estates was formed at the beginning of the seventeenth century which retained separate entities although their owners have changed. In one part of the Strath, the slope down which Mitchell's road runs to the river, the old plough-gate of Raigmore and some adjacent land have sometimes been joined to Clune, or held separately by lease or some indefinite tenure, the superiority of the land being held by Grant of Dalvey. In 1702 Raigmore was bought by Mackintosh of Borlum. His family was influential in Strathdearn and is unique in the very diverse characters of different members of it.

William Mackintosh of Borlum, famous as 'the Old Brigadier', was the eldest son of Mackintosh of Borlum. He was head of an ancient branch of the clan which occupied the valuable lands of Borlum in the valley of the river Ness, and also of Raits (now called Balavil) in

Badenoch. William graduated from Kings College, Aberdeen in 1677. He saw a little military service, but was much in London and married a Maid of Honour to Princess Anne, afterwards Queen of England. She belonged to a loyalist family and he seems to have remained in the South until after the Revolution when he served in James VII's campaign in Ireland and in Bonnie Dundee's Rising in Scotland. Because of his Jacobite activities his father prudently settled Borlum on Lachlan, William's son, and Raits on his wife.

In 1698 William settled at Raits. Having seen more advanced methods of agriculture in England, he tried with all the intensity of his nature to improve the deplorable methods of agriculture in the Highlands. In his old age, in his *Essay*, his mind turned back to this happy period of his life and he told how he sowed a row of ash trees on the slope below the house of Balavil in 1715 before he was summoned to join Clan Mackintosh for the Rising. (Their decrepit remains were still there when I came to Kingussie to form the Folk Museum.) He had already been active in organizing support for the Jacobite cause. He joined the march to Inverness, where Mackintosh of Mackintosh publicly proclaimed James VIII as King, and to Perth to join forces with the Earl of Mar.

From then onwards, although he was advanced to the rank of Brigadier, William was at constant loggerheads with the indecision, differences of opinion and general inefficiency of the Jacobite commander. He had a brief interlude of independent action when he was given command of an expedition sent to test whether Edinburgh would rise in the Jacobite cause. He and most of his men made a daring crossing of the mouth of the Firth of Forth, while the Hanoverians were watching Burntisland, but Argyll, the efficient Hanoverian commander, had hastened to protect Edinburgh and he rejoined the Jacobite army. The dither of complicity and vacillating counsels continued and a bystander wrote of the Brigadier's 'grim countenance'. The melancholy story of the occupation of Preston, its siege and surrender, continued with here and there a mention of the Brigadier's protests.

After the surrender the leading men, including Mackintosh of Mackintosh and two or three members of his clan, the Brigadier among them, were sent to London for trial for high treason. They were all marched through the streets of London surrounded by a jeering mob, but we are told that the Brigadier 'remarkable for the grim ferocity of his scarred face' excited more respect than ridicule. The Brigadier was among the prisoners who were lodged in Newgate to await their trial.

One of them escaped and the others were put in irons. The Brigadier, on the very evening before his trial, 'found means to get rid of his irons', came downstairs and stood behind the door of the prison so that, when it was opened, he was able to rush out, knocking down the turnkey and making his escape, breaking past several guards and snatching the bayonet of one of them. Several other prisoners also managed to get away with him.

The Londoners were delighted at the daring escape on the very eve of the solemnities of a trial for high treason and the Brigadier was the hero of a popular ballad:

> Brave Derwentwater he is dead,
> From his fair body they took the head;
> But Mackintosh and his friends are fled,
> And they'll set the hat on another head
> And whether they're gone beyond the sea
> Or if they abide in this countree
> Tho' our King would give ten thousand pounds,
> Old Mackintosh would scorn to be found.

A reward of £1000 was offered for his capture and he was described as a tall raw-boned man of about sixty, beetle-browed, of fair complexion.

Good friends to the cause must have given him help. He made his way to Oxfordshire, where he hid in waste country near his brother-in-law's home, and then escaped to the continent. He was back in the Highlands to take part in the abortive rising in 1719. In the battle of Glen Shiel he was posted with the Spanish troops but, although they were forced to surrender, he managed to escape and, after hiding in the Highlands for a short time, he was able to return to France.

During the next few years he seems to have lived in France, sometimes visiting Scotland on Jacobite business. A letter survived, written to him in 1722 by the Old Chevalier, the sovereign that he served so devotedly. From it one gathers that he was enduring hardships. Then, although the £1000 was still offered for his capture and he was an outlaw, he returned to his old home at Raits.

It is evident that family affairs had brought him home. It will be remembered that, to safeguard the family inheritance, his father had left Borlum to the Brigadier's son, Lachlan, and Raits to his wife. Both his father and his wife had died and so his son, Lachlan, had inherited both properties. He had emigrated to America, married there and died leaving two daughters. Lachlan's wife had also apparently died. The Brigadier had also had a younger son, named Shaw, who had wished to obtain possession of the property. He had gone to America to try to get possession of the little heiress and her sister. He at first had posed as their kind uncle but, failing to obtain possession of them, he had then tried to kidnap them. He was foiled, nearly lynched and imprisoned at Boston till he gave a bond of £2000 not to molest them. When the Brigadier returned, he was occupying Raits. No record survives of how the Brigadier's family had been cared for while he devoted his energies to the Jacobite cause and it was, of course, at great personal risk that he came back to his old home. It was given out that he was Shaw's cousin.

Of course, the authorities were on the watch for the return of the wanted rebel to his old haunts and when Lieutenant Harris, the Officer in Command at Ruthven Barracks, heard of the presence of Shaw's 'cousin' at Raits he sent word and a messenger with a warrant for his arrest was sent up from London. Shaw was apparently absent at the time, but Lieutenant Harris sent his servant to Raits to say that he would be shooting in the vicinity and would be glad 'to take a breakfast' with Mackintosh's cousin. The Brigadier was in bed when the servant arrived but he rose at once and 'in his dressing gown and slippers' received Lieutenant Harris who arrived immediately afterwards. They sat chatting and suddenly the messenger, accompanied by six soldiers, entered the room and Lieutenant Harris informed the Brigadier that he was the King's prisoner. The Brigadier made no resistance but asked if he could go to his room to dress. This was refused and Shaw (who may never really have been absent from Raits) suddenly appeared in the story and was also arrested.

By this time a crowd of country people, whose suspicions had been aroused by the presence of the soldiers, was gathering outside the house and Lieutenant Harris threatened the prisoners that 'if a rescue was attempted they were dead men'. Shaw and the messenger were then sent to try to disperse the crowd but, while they were trying to do so, some numbers of the crowd burst into the house and others seized the messenger. Shaw tried to save him and, in a rough-and-tumble struggle, he was wounded. Meanwhile the Old Brigadier made his escape. The angry authorities took it out on Shaw who was taken to London and tried for high treason.

For three years more the Brigadier remained at large. Finally in 1727 he was captured or gave himself up. He was penniless and the officer who arrested him reported that he, himself, had to pay for Mackintosh's food on the way and that he would die of want if public help was not given. He was imprisoned in Edinburgh Castle. No proceedings seem to have been taken against him but he remained a prisoner for fifteen years until his death in 1743. If he had renounced his loyalty to the House of Stuart one wonders if he might not have received a royal pardon, but his loyalty was unwavering until the day of his death.

It was in the days of his imprisonment that he revealed the most surprising and endearing side of his character. His mind turned back to his interests and ambitions, in the happy days of his family life at Raits, and his plans to introduce better ways of farming and to increase the fertility of the lands and plant the barren wastes.

In 1729 he wrote *An Essay on Ways and Means for Inclosing Fallowing and Planting in Scotland and that in sixteen years at the Fairthest* – by 'A Lover of his Country'. In this remarkable essay he began by blaming, in very strong words, the evils of tenancy at will, emphasizing that the landlord, under the system, had undue power; he could remove a tenant at his whim and that therefore the tenant had no incentive to improve his holding. He stated, 'It is just, it is human, it is what religion requires of us,' that the tenants of Scotland should have the right to pay their rent as any landlord has to receive it. He said that it was his object to make from a poor a rich, from an ugly and inconvenient, a happy, beautiful and commodious country. He advocated the setting up of an Agricultural College, and that the state should exercise more power in the promotion of good agriculture, especially by means of education. He advocated state help to encourage the cultivation of flax and farming of sheep, and drastic reform of the existing policy on fisheries. He emphasized the need for encouraging home manufacturers and condemned the fashion for foreign novelties.[27]

This is the first of many associations with the struggle to restore the Stuarts to the British throne that one meets with in following our bit of the road. Because it most deeply affected the lives of the people of Strathdearn, I am often surprised at the comparative lack of interest people now show in Jacobite stories and traditions. When I was young it was a matter of great personal pride if one's forebears had fought at Culloden and been 'out' in the '15. Two generations earlier, Jacobite sympathies were even stronger – although at the same time there was unquestioning loyalty to Queen Victoria. For instance, Mary Mackintosh of Raigmore told me that once she went to fetch the Jacobite relics in her family to show to an old lady and that, when she entered the room carrying them, the old lady stood up and made a deep curtsey. Mr Ramsay Biscoe of Newton, a contemporary of my father, said that when he was young he was at a dinner party at Beaufort at which Charles Sobieski Stuart was the guest of honour. It will be remembered that the two Sobieski Stuart brothers claimed that they were the legitimate grandsons of Prince Charles Edward. This was accepted by a number of Scotsmen, including Lord Lovat, and disbelieved by a number of others. The brothers visited the Highlands many times about the middle of the last century and the authenticity of their claim was a burning matter of dispute in Highland society. Several people have told me that, in their youth, they had been told of the brothers' strong facial resemblance to Prince Charlie and how they played up to it. At the dinner party Charles Sobieski Stuart accidentally jogged the arm of the footman just as he was serving the lady sitting next to him with a plate of soup and the footman spilled some of it on her dress. Sobieski Stuart was profuse in his apologies and begged her to let him have the dress cleaned and she replied: 'Never would she wish the dress to be cleaned over which her rightful King had spilled the soup.'

To return to the Brigadier's family connection with Raigmore – the Brigadier's son, Shaw, was a worthless spend-thrift who dissipated the family inheritance, and his son was the highwayman whom I mentioned in my account of Wade's road. But the Brigadier's younger brother, Joseph, had bought Raigmore, a small property on the march of Clune, from Grant of Dalvey. I have always understood that he built the house about 1702. His son, Lachlan, went to India, made a fortune, came home and bought land on Nairnside and part of the Castlehill property on the outskirts of Inverness. He transferred to this land the name of Raigmore and made it his home. His son, Aeneas, sat for a time as MP for Inverness-shire. He was a leading man in the district and, among other activities, was one of the chief supporters for the project of building the railway from Perth to Inverness. His three daughters, the last representatives of this strangely diverse line, lived very quietly in their beautiful house on the outskirts of Inverness. They worked hard to further every good cause in Inverness. They were close friends of my mother, they were always kind and hospitable to me and I knew the house and its fine policies well. I have never felt so old as when I happened to revisit that district and saw that a hospital and housing estate covered their land, and all that was left of the old Raigmore was one of the holly trees that stood at the back door.

5

The Land and the People

A Changed Way of Farming

The change in the look of the farmland is an obvious sign of how greatly life in the Strath has altered during the last two hundred years. I have hitherto adopted the style of a raconteuse in my treatment of the subject matter but, because the history of rural life in the Highlands has become a subject of great bitterness of feeling, I am anxious to state the sources and give the facts as fully as I can in writing about it.

By about the middle of the eighteenth century the old group of cattle-farming proprietors were taking up other professions. They had given up their holdings in the lower lands of Moray, on which they had wintered their cattle, and all but two of them were sooner or later to sell their estates. More gradually, farms cultivated by the groups of joint farmers or tenants were to be succeeded by self-supporting hill farms, farmed by individual tenant farmers. These local agrarian adjustments were part of radical changes going on all over the country and were so great and so closely associated that the whole process has become known as the Agricultural Revolution.

In Strathdearn most of the great changes came about very gradually. The minister of the parish wrote in 1793 that they had hardly begun and his successor in 1836 was to declare that 'there is perhaps not a parish in Scotland which has undergone less change than this'.

Nevertheless, even at the time when the first minister was writing, one great change had already taken place. He noted the introduction of the hardy black-faced sheep. This was one of two reasons for the replacement of the extensive rearing of cattle by that of sheep. In 1792-3 the number of black cattle in the parish was said to be 1800, and that of sheep 12,000.[1] When one remembers that the population of the parish at that time was over 1800 and that all the milk and butter, an important part of the people's diet, was home-produced, this number of cattle (of all ages) strikes one as quite small. Of course, since the Second World War the position has again changed and milk and butter are bought at the shop. A great deal of work is saved and also the tie of regular milking times. On the other hand, milch cows are interesting animals to look after and, in the old days, for a cottager to be able to keep a cow was quite a status symbol. When my grandmother came to live at Balnespick, a local girl used to work in the house when special help was needed. She lived with a married brother; my grandmother thought she was treated as a drudge and was sorry for her. But one day she suddenly said: 'I am getting a cow.' Grannie was surprised but supposed that the brother would let it pasture with his own stock. 'Oh no,' the girl replied, 'I'm getting grazing for her.' Grannie, still more surprised, asked where she would keep the cow. 'I'm getting a byre for her,' answered the girl and added: 'I'm getting a man.' She was making a very good match.

The minister in the *Old Statistical Account* records that 'of late some parts of the parish which contained a great number of inhabitants, have been laid out in sheep farms, which had diminished the population very considerably'. (As a matter of fact since 1755, if Webster's estimate is correct, the population had increased from 1693 to 1813 souls.) 'Clearing' is also stated to have taken place in the *New Statistical Account*[2] and there had been one case (at Corriebrough) where the estate had been sold, entirely cleared of the people cultivating it by the purchaser, a land surveyor called Campbell Smith, and made into a sheep farm.[3] But areas in Strathdearn are relatively small compared to those cleared in Sutherland and Ross-shire and none of the other dozen or so properties in which it was divided were cleared in this wholesale fashion.

On the contrary, the introduction of the hardy black-faced sheep did not lead to a complete depopulation of the district and the formation of vast sheep walks because, unlike the cattle, these sheep could thrive on the nearby heathery hills in the summer, as well as on the remoter shielings, and in winter could be maintained on the produce of an upland farm. It was they who made the small hill farms, that were then coming into existence in many parts of the Highlands, a viable proposition.

The second great change that affected the agriculture of the Highlands at about this time was the rising market value of grain production, due to the long series of continental wars that reached a climax in the Napoleonic struggle. This was an incentive for improving the fertility of

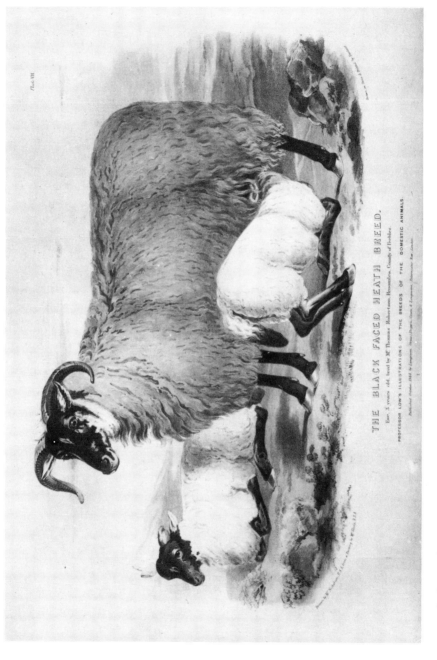

Plate VII.

THE BLACK FACED HEATH BREED.

Ewe 3 years old, bred by Mr Thomas Robertson, Braxmire, County of Peebles.

PROFESSOR LOW'S ILLUSTRATIONS OF THE BREEDS OF THE DOMESTIC ANIMALS.

Published October 1842 by Longman, Orme, Brown, Green & Longmans, Paternoster Row, London.

Black Faced or Linton Breed of Sheep. From David Low, *The Breeds of the Domestic Animals of the British Isles.*

the soil by field drainage and the addition of lime or other materials.

In Strathdearn, most of the farmland lies along the river and at the foot of steep hillsides – it must largely be due to field drainage that the best of it has been reclaimed from marsh. This is especially noticeable at Dell, a farm a little above the bridge on the left side of the river. Another probable instance of early field drainage is on the farm at Invereen. The arable land of this farm lies along the banks of the Findhorn and at the mouth of its tributary, the Funtack. This low-lying land is enclosed by long steep banks. Early and skilful use of field drainage has probably rescued the fields from marsh and the wide ditch which was built to prevent water seeping down the hillsides is still evident. The family of Dunbar came to Strathdearn in 1720 from Auldearn on the Morayshire coast where agriculture was much more advanced. Murdo MacAskill noticed similar but smaller improvements to individual farms all over Strathdearn.

I was lucky enough to see an old field-drain that had been made long before the introduction of the modern method of tile-drainage. It is not in Strathdearn but at Dunachton in Badenoch which my forebear farmed in the 1760s. He was evidently a bit of an innovator and he made many references in his diary to the making of a field-drain. When I was writing a book, founded on his diary, I bicycled the twenty odd miles to see Dunachton. I identified the field on a slope close to the ruined chapel *down* which the drain had been made. Some men were at work in the middle of the field digging a trench to lay a tile-drain *across* it. They had obviously found something interesting and when I went to look I saw that it was the old, old drain made of stones carefully fitted together to form a channel. It was a piece of good fortune that I should have been there at the brief time when the trench for the new drain crossed the line of the old one.

The application of lime was an early improvement that Strathdearn was very slow to take up. According to the *New Statistical Account* it was costly to buy and little used there, but very shortly after the account was written (in the late 1830s and early 1840s) it was being made at Kyllachie.

The most essential feature of the agricultural reforms was the growing of a regular rotation of crops including, in addition to cereals, sown hay, a fallow and turnips. Like field drainage and, to some extent, the use of lime, the cultivation of a rotation of crops would be extremely difficult to work by groups of joint tenants and a new pattern of land-holding was evolved in order to carry it on.

View up Strathdearn from the Viaduct.

This process of conversion from large-scale cattle raising and jointly cultivated farms to single, moderately sized holdings cultivated on the reformed methods of cultivation, was carried out over a large area of the Highlands by three great landowners: the Duke of Argyll, the Duke of Gordon and the Laird of Grant, as well as by many lesser ones. It was my good luck to learn about the process and its results from people deeply versed in the relative documents and with first-hand experience: George Dixon, Margaret Gerrard, Eric Cregeen and Hope MacDougall. I was equally fortunate in having the help of people with on-the-spot experience: Murdo MacAskill and my brother and nephew. Relating all this to local farming traditions, I venture to reconstruct the story of what happened in Strathdearn.

According to the *Old Statistical Account* of 1792-3, there had been little improvement although the people all grew some potatoes. Of the proprietors, Sheriff MacQueen of Corriebrough, farmed his land but, according to Sir Aeneas Mackintosh, it was 'unenclosed', whereas William Mackintosh of Clune and Balnespick, whose grandfather had made the field-drain at Dunachton that I visited, was himself a keen agricultural reformer on his farm at Clune. In 1804 he was presented with a beautiful silver cup by the Badenoch and Strath Spey Farming Society 'for having the best turnip crop in the district'.

To make a digression from a dry subject, this presentation brings us into touch with a most colourful personality. The Strath Spey Farming Society had been formed one year previously by Jane Duchess of Gordon and the minister of the parish. The Duchess is commemorated by an obelisk at Kinrara for all the good work she did in the district. She cut a somewhat striking figure and is best remembered for recruiting for the Gordon Highlanders by holding 'the King's Shilling' between her teeth.

Progress, however, was slow. According to the estimate of the value of the produce of Strathdearn in the *New Statistical Account* (1836) the total value of potatoes (of which everyone grew a few) and turnips was £700 and that of hay (that all-important crop that preceded the fallow) £225. Whereas the grain produced was valued at £5640, the output of wool was valued at £700 and pasturage for sheep £1333. Pasturage for cattle was valued at £822.[4] The value of the cattle and sheep sold is not given but one must remember that, at this period, large-scale sheep farming was mainly carried out for the production of wool, although some delicious three-year-old wedder mutton might be given to a friend or sold locally, as a gastronomic treat. Charles St John, who gives many a valuable sidelight upon nineteenth-century Highland life in his *Wild Sports and Natural History of the Highlands* (1846) is not complimentary about the farming of Strathdearn. On a walk down it he commented that the peat stacks were larger than the farmhouses. (But he also noticed the hospitable welcome that he received if he entered any of them.) The corn was standing green and uncut while it was harvest time in the Laich of Moray.[5]

The *New Statistical Account* gives a hint of what was taking place when it states that quite a number of nineteen-year leases of farms, provided with adequate farm steadings, had been granted. Local history tells us who got them. About the 1820s a family of seven brothers named Macgillivray, were tenants of seven farms in Strathdearn. One of them rented Dell and it was probably he who drained its low-lying fields. William Mackintosh of Clune and Balnespick had died and my grand-father was very young when he succeeded him, which accounts for two Macgillivrays taking over the farms of Clune and Balmore (evidently the old steading of Balnespick). The farm at Free had been tenanted by the father of the brothers. Garbole is said to have been a part of Morile. Probably the farms that the remaining brothers tenanted (Morile and Auchnagael) had been the home farms of old farming proprietors.

The brothers were not intruders from outside but came of influential local stock. Their mother was the daughter of Donald Macpherson, one of the 'Five Godly Donalds' whom I have already mentioned. Their father was Finlay Macgillivray, tenant of Free (a small estate absorbed by Tomatin) and said in his day to have been one of three most influential men in Strathdearn. They were therefore known as the Clan Unela = *Clann Fhionnlaigh* = the Children of Finlay. It would be interesting to know if they had had any experience of the improved method outside Strathdearn, but a talent for farming seems to have been in their blood for all their descendants eventually moved to better farms elsewhere, the most outstanding member of them being Captain John Macgillivray of Pullrossie, the breeder of a famous breed of short-horns.

The change to the new methods of agriculture came more slowly on other farms. In 1811 we learn that there were eleven holdings in Corriebrough and in eight of them there was joint occupancy by two tenants.[6] When I was young, the Nobles, who rented Upper Inverbrough on Balnespick, had reminiscences of when their family shared the farm with another tenant, and I remember seeing the foundations of a second house above the present steading. I am fairly sure that two other farms on Balnespick were farmed by two joint tenants. At one stage Morile (on

Kyllachie) was held by two tenants and their shares were demarcated. Such joint tenancies may have occurred elsewhere; for instance, there were evidently still four joint tenants at Woodend when Mr MacAskill's grandmother was young.

There was evidently great variation in the change from joint to single tenancies in different districts, as the Argyll estate papers show. Mr Cregeen compares the reorganization of the holdings in the Kintyre part of the estate with my description of Strathdearn. Between 1779 and 1800 the average number of tenants on twenty-five farms had dropped from over four to less than three and their holdings had been consolidated and were no longer in scattered rigs.

According to the *New Statistical Account* the land usually held was 'ridge about', as it is called, and, after a series of crops, the land is left for a year in 'ley'; on this most of the available manure was spread. Black oats (an inferior variety) was still the main crop.[7] This at least was an advance on the old infield and outfield, but it is rather surprising to find how slowly the improvements were coming about.

It is obvious that one of the first steps in improving a farm would be to level the rigs. This comes out strongly in the fascinatingly circumstantial account of the reforms on the farms on the island of Kerrera.[8] In the Seafield Papers also there are accounts of payment for levelling the land[9] but no local accounts of the actual expense involved. We know that before the *New Statistical Account* was written there were at least eight farms, probably more, in single occupation and that joint tenancy by two tenants was frequent.

During the period between the two accounts there had been a marked drop in the population of the parish of Strathdearn. In 1793 it had been 1813. In 1831 it was 1098. The acreage under cultivation had evidently not been diminished. According to the *New Statistical Account* it was 2820 acres, largely outshot, and the only additional available land was said to be fit solely for outfield, so good land cannot have been lost to cultivation between the two accounts.

Agriculture was the only source of livelihood and yet there were said to be 200 farmers' houses and 340 cottagers and, to work the land and serve the needs of the community, not fewer than 246 ploughs and 900 horses were kept. In our severe and unreliable climate it is little wonder that only in favourable years was the produce of the district even 'nearly' equal to the consumption of the parish.[10] Until the eighteenth century it was virtually impossible for any but the sons of the more affluent landholders to leave the country and find a livelihood elsewhere. One becomes acutely conscious of this in studying the genealogies of the lesser gentry and the younger sons of even the magnates, and of the liberation that they experienced when the eighteenth century provided them with wider opportunities. This must have applied even more strongly to the lesser folk.

Yet in deploring the poverty of the people within the limited confines of the arid Highland glens, one's admiration grows for the lives they made for themselves – shot through with music, poetry and an oral tradition of magnificent epics of which we merely transcribe the surviving fragments, and of the distinction of their manners and diction, the very appreciation of which has been almost lost. The French traveller, Louis Simond, has *le mot juste* when he wrote that the people had a 'superiority to want'.[11]

In 1836 there were only 212 houses; cottages are not mentioned although farm servants were employed on the larger farms.[12] The people were said still to be mainly employed in agriculture and the minister noted that the congregations at Dalarossie, the more rural end of the Strath, were larger than at Moy. Although there had been great improvements in the implements used – notably in the introduction of efficient ploughs pulled by two horses, agriculture was still exceedingly laborious. Corn was cut with the sickle and threshed by the flail, the need for constant herding was increased when better crops were grown. For their fuel supply, people were entirely dependent upon peat which they themselves had to cut, dry and carry. One is thankful that the standard of living had to some extent risen. In the *New Statistical Account* the minister wrote that 'the people generally live comfortably considering their station. They have bread, potatoes, milk, butter and cheese and many of them [have] animal food.'[13]

Against this background of gradual change I have been privileged to set Mr Murdo MacAskill's recollections of his grandmother. Margaret Macpherson's father was the son of Donald Macpherson, one of the 'Five Godly Donalds'. She was, therefore, the kinswoman of the prosperous Clan Unela. Her father was not so successful from a worldly point of view, although he had the nickname 'strong' and must have transmitted to her his magnificent physique. When he died in 1860 Margaret – or 'Mickie Vohr' as using phonetic spelling her name is written – had to support her mother on 'half the grass' of a cow. They had the occupation of a house at Woodend Farm and it is evident that her mother had

Ploughing at Corriebrough. Photograph in Sir W. Malkin's Papers.

inherited this from her father, a Cattanach, who had been a joint tenant on the farm. Mickie Vohr evidently took part in all the collective work that was still done on an old-fashioned farm. She was quicker and better than anyone else in the band of women harvesters who gathered the corn into sheaves and stooked them.

She was full of spirit. One day she and some friends walked to market in Inverness (fourteen miles) and on the way back, at the Black Wood near Moy, they were accosted by a man on horseback, a carrier named Haldane, who was suspected, rightly, as it was afterwards proved, of murdering two girls on their way back from harvest work in the South. Mickie Vohr stood up to him. She, in Mr MacAskill's words 'struck his horse a hefty blow on the rump with her stick and Haldane troubled the party no more'.

With her splendid strength, Mickie Vohr earned money, in an unusual way, to support her mother. She cut, lifted and led home large quantities of peat, most of which she used in making lime. While engaged in hauling limestone from the quarry high above the present house of Kyllachie she met, and later married, an incomer from Harris named MacAskill who worked there. It took twelve loads of peat and the same of limestone to load the kiln which burned for three days and had to be tended through two nights. It must have been exhausting work but her life had its compensations. Her grandson commented, 'I have often thought that my grandparents had a very comfortable courting place.' They married and lived with her mother at Woodend. They had to leave when she died and they found a tumbledown house and made it comfortable. Then, in 1877, her husband died, leaving her to fend for herself and four young children between the ages of two and eleven years. The little family was almost entirely dressed in knitted garments made from wool of her own spinning. She smoked the hams of sheep killed by braxy and her better-off relations gave her small quantities of oats. The children went out to herd at nine years of age. She also went out to work for some of these cousins. After the washing-day at Garbole, which in the old Scots custom took place every three months, her knuckles were red and bleeding from scrubbing the coarse-knitted socks and underwear.

She reared her family and, in her old age, went to live with her married daughter. She had kept her spirit and keen wits and when the new Laird of Kyllachie, a distinguished advocate who had just been made a judge with the title of Lord Kyllachie, came to call she was able to hold her own in a lively argument over his right to preserve the salmon fishing.

She finally insisted on going back to the old home she and her husband had made habitable and she died there in 1920. Mickie Vohr grew up and lived in a society with a very definite pattern. It was made up of farmers on small upland sheep farms into which, long before my days, the jointly held farms had developed. Of the surnames, nearly all of these farmers – Macgillivray, Mackintosh, Macbean, MacQueen, Macpherson – were clans belonging to Clan Chattan and their descent could be traced more or less definitely to families who had been settled in the district for centuries. The Nobles had been in the district a long time. The Dunbars had come to Strathdearn in 1720 but can trace their descent from one of the great families in the Laich of Moray.

I can remember how Annie Noble, who like all good Highlanders was a born genealogist, could reel off the descent and intermarriages of most of the residents in the Strath. Mr MacAskill can do the same and draw up a chart of the ramifications of his relationships. The Macdonalds and the Frasers came later to the Strath and have merged into the group. Two other people with long associations with the district, men of great personal distinction, were Mr Davidson at Bridge of Findhorn, whose people had been on Dunachton in my own forebears' days there and had come with them to Strathdearn, and Mr Fraser, the direct descendant of the blacksmith of Moy, the 'Captain of Five'.

In Mickie Vohr's lifetime the terrible dearth of the late 1840s brought many losses to everyone connected with agriculture and privation to those who were still subsistence farmers. The suffering cannot have been so acute as in previous dearths when the Strath was more isolated and limited to its own resources but, as an integral part of the wider community, it was to bear its full share in the suffering brought about by two great changes in agricultural economy.

About the middle of the century, the sheep farmers suffered a devastating blow from the competition of superior wool from Australia. Then the transport of frozen meat hit the raising of cattle as well as of sheep almost as severe a blow. However, the upland sheep farmers have adjusted their methods to counter the latter. They have concentrated their efforts upon the production of mutton from their year-old stock. The produce of the farm has become more and more entirely devoted to the provision of winter feeding for the sheep although the valuable young stock is now sent to the low ground for wintering. The sale of wool has become of secondary importance.

After the 1860s, wire fences came into use to divide the various fields and constant herding ceased to be necessary. When I was young, many of the older people remembered long days of their childhood spent in herding and generally the memories were happy ones. Till the Second World War one always saw a dairy cow or two pasturing among the other stock. Nowadays I do not think that one could be seen as all the milk is supplied in glass bottles from dairies near Inverness. For many years there were even a few cattle beasts on a good many of the farms but now the raising of beef cattle is carried on by a few men with capital.

A change with more momentous implications is the disappearance of all the work horses. Now agricultural machinery has taken over. This has involved more capitalization and often a different type of farmer, with a diminution in their numbers. The remuneration and the qualifications of farm workers have changed. The communal activities at harvest, sheep-shearing, etc., have been lost to the people of the Strath. More important than the changes in stock or land is that in population. In Strathdearn it is impossible to tell how far the decrease was voluntary. In other parts of the country written records have survived showing that emigration to America started before large-scale sheep farming and was then unwelcome to the lairds and tacksmen.[14]

Some local men are known to have joined Selkirk's planned emigration. Large numbers must have enlisted after Pitt made his famous boast in the House of Commons that, by his statesmanship, he had made available the fighting power of the Highlander for the defence of the country. Regiment after regiment was raised, especially during the Napoleonic Wars. For instance, in 1754, less than a decade after the carnage at Culloden, 500 Mackintosh clansmen enlisted in the 42nd Regiment in which Mackintosh held a commission,[15] and when many members of the lesser gentry obtained commissions in the army, no doubt they enlisted a quota of men from the family estates.

It has been the young, the enterprising, the flower of our manhood who have fared forth. The writer of the *New Statistical Account* lamented this in 1836 at some length, complaining that the young men 'are all leaving us for the New World', and so it has gone on. Although both he and his predecessor in the *Old Statistical Account* complained that there had been some clearances, the only large-scale one recorded is the 'clearing'

Sheep Shearing, as late as 1960 neighbours gathered to lend a hand and were entertained by the farmer. Photograph in Sir W. Malkin's Papers.

of the whole of the medium-sized estate of Corriebrough. The joint tenants of eleven holdings were evicted and went to America, the new owner being Campbell Smith. He made the whole estate into a sheep farm which one is glad to think was not very successful.[16] The memory of some displaced people on other individual farms also lingers on. When so many estates changed hands and when still more farms, each cultivated by several joint farmers with their cottages, were divided into holdings formed by a single tenant, some dislocation could hardly have been avoided.

The Moors and the Lodges

Closing in the Strath upon either side are the grouse moors. Financially and socially they are now of great importance. I feel that I ought to give some account of the people who shot over them, as I remember them, because that section of society has almost vanished and so their way of life is worth recording. It was one facet in the many sides of country life one used to get in the close intermingling of people with different backgrounds in one's ordinary daily comings and goings when living in the country.

Grouse shooting for sport is not a very old institution. It cannot have been easy to shoot winged game with the ancient matchlock guns and it was only done for the pot and not for sport. In the nineteenth century the flintlock fowling piece was improved and shooting became a fashionable sport in England.[17] The flintlock was affected by rain or damp which would be of special disadvantage on a Highland moor. It was not, therefore, until the end of the eighteenth century or the very early part of the nineteenth century that anyone thought of preserving the shooting on grouse moors. Land that had been valueless for pasturing cattle, and only useful for feeding the hardiest breed of sheep for part of the year only, gradually became the most valuable asset of a Highland estate.

About the beginning of the nineteenth century gentlemen began to go grouse shooting and landowners would give them permission to shoot over their land. The game had to be walked up and was a sport for the active and popular with officers stationed in Scotland. With the flintlock muzzle-loading guns of the day, almost always with only one barrel, it must have called for dexterity as well as marksmanship. It was recorded as a great exploit that the brother of Lord Moray shot eighty brace in one day;[18] there is a tradition that William Mackintosh (my great-grand-

On the Way to the Moor. Sketch by Canon W.L. Mackintosh.

father) shot a hundred brace in a day for a wager. A local poet, recording it in verse, likened William Mackintosh to Finn MacCoul, the leader of the Feinné; he then continued, 'It was pleasant to Thee to be traversing the soaring hills, with thy pretty gun that would not refuse.' He added that the smith had oiled it carefully, 'When it would burn the powder, and thou wouldst wink with thine eye towards the ark.'[19]

Great improvements were made in the design of fowling pieces during the early part of the nineteenth century. The flintlock was superseded by the percussion cap. Shooting birds on the wing became easier and the effects of damp were eliminated.

In the 1820s the percussion cap was in general use. Shooting birds on the wing became fashionable and before this, in 1816 'Saxon gentlemen' had 'caught the heather mania'.[20] There is a story that in 1820 Mackintosh let Coignafearn (one of the finest moors in the district) for £20 and he was surprised at getting so much for a 'few hens'.

Before the 1840s shootings in Strathdearn were beginning to be let and shooting lodges of a simple kind were built or existing farm houses adapted. This was the case at Corriebrough and probably at Balnespick. Square two-storied houses with four rooms, and perhaps garrets, were the stock pattern. Balnespick was let for the shooting. Clune also was let to two sportsmen, but my grandfather, before he went to India, must have stayed there for my mother had a story that, whenever the tenants complained about anything to the old woman who was caretaker and 'did' for them, she would reply: 'Set you up to complain of that when himself was well satisfied?' By 1850 there were shooting lodges at Glen Mazeran and Dalmigavie. A shooting lodge had been built at Kyllachie about 1844 but, when the estate became the permanent home of the proprietor, it was largely rebuilt in a more imposing form by W.L. Carruthers, an Inverness firm of architects who were responsible for most of the local lodges of this period. It was again added to in 1894.

In 1845 Mr Malkin had bought Corriebrough and, from the 1850s onwards, the reminiscences collected by his great-great-nephew's wife, Margaret Malkin, neatly fitted into and confirmed what scraps of information I can remember hearing about or saw actually happening. In the case of this group of good but medium-sized grouse moors in the middle of Strathdearn, their owners and shooting tenants were largely soldiers, members of the higher branches of the Law and Colonial Services, and business people with much the same or a rather more affluent style of living. This pattern did not change in essentials between

Corriebrough House – a much added to Shooting Lodge.

the middle of the nineteenth century and the First World War. On larger moors, such as those owned by Mackintosh and Lord Cawdor, the tenants were, of course, much richer men and their style of living was different. The actual guns used were much improved about the late 1840s and early fifties by the introduction of cartridges and of breech instead of muzzle loading.

In Strathdearn, until about the 1890s, shooting was over dogs and the birds were walked up. I am told that further north it is still the custom. The number of guns was not large, three or four or half a dozen. They walked in line, quartering the most likely parts of the moor, the pointers or setters, generally one dog at a time, working to and fro and covering the ground in front of them. When a dog scented a covey of grouse in the heather, he slowed down, his tail becoming rigidly straight and, pointing at the game, he advanced very slowly. The two guns nearest to him began to converge. The dog, ever more rigid, slowed down. He almost stopped. The guns on full alert moved forward. Excitement mounted. Almost at the same moment that the dog stopped, the covey with a loud whirring of wings, seemed to burst from the heather. The guns fired, a bird or two dropped and some downy feathers floated away. The keeper, who had walked behind the guns and more or less tactfully suggested the line of operations, stepped forward and his retriever (certainly not a labrador, and in earlier days, a retriever with a coat of tight little black curls that I can just remember) bounded forward to find and bring back the fallen birds. Still more in the background was a pony with panniers. As a small girl I have viewed such shoots from inside one of the panniers when grouse shooting was a simpler informal affair. Ladies, if they did accompany the guns, generally rode a pony. In the 1890s, with the introduction of that female liberator, the bicycle, women wore clothes more suitable for the country, and skirts of a more practical length were worn then. By the time my age had got into double figures, women would sometimes walk behind the guns.

All this time, grouse moors were becoming more and more valuable as grouse shooting increased in prestige; shooting lodges became larger or had extensions built onto them. At Balnespick a wing was added, including the servants hall — a stock term for a very ordinary apartment. In many cases, a row of rooms built of corrugated iron had to be built onto the lodges to accommodate more guns as a change came over the method of shooting. As an important addition to walking up the birds it became the fashion, later in the season, to drive them over a line of butts.

Driving Grouse. Sketch by Canon W.L. Mackintosh, one-time Rector of St Michael's Inverness.

POINTER BITCH "BELLE," THE PROPERTY OF MR. R. J. LLOYD PRICE.

Pointer.
Flat-coated and Curly Retrievers. From Vera Shaw, *The Illustrated Book of the Dog*.

Until the Second World War shooting tenants with their house parties occupied the lodges for a whole season, although the engagement of the requisite staff became an increasing difficulty.

After the Second World War, as people came up for shorter times, their activities became more and more concentrated on these drives. Driving was expensive and it brought a shower of welcome small payments to a great many children and people with spare time to act as beaters.

I saw much less of the new way of shooting for family reasons. Two memories stick in my mind. The people who were renting Balnespick very kindly asked me to join the house party for a day on the hill. My father had died and, as the custom then was, I was wearing deep mourning. In mood, circumstances and clothes I felt out of touch with the other people. They were affluent and generous and I noticed how well the gentlemen tipped the beaters and ghillies for any small service. Paper money did not so lightly change hands in these days. Yet when the guns and other guests gathered for lunch and the beaters went off for theirs, every one of the beaters who had happened to pick a bit of white heather as he walked over the moor brought it to me, whom they knew had nothing with which to tip them.

The shooting tenant at Glenkirk (part of Corriebrough) for about thirty years, the Rev. E.L. Browne, the headmaster of a school at Eastbourne, had the unique distinction of having a memorial erected to his memory by the country people. He was immensely popular but I remember him because he used poodles instead of retrievers. My brother, who shot with him several times, said that they were very intelligent and good workers but that they had not such soft mouths as retrievers.

I was only a relation of the landowners and I do not know what their incomes were, but one was very much aware of the increasing importance of the shootings. As agriculture could never be very remunerative in such a high upland strath, less fertile farms became vacant, the cost of fencing and maintenance increased and only the shooting rents went up. The heathery hillsides which, apart from the distant shielings, had been valueless for rearing cattle and could only provide summer grazing for the black-faced sheep, became increasingly the most remunerative part of an estate and a useful source of employment.

By the kindness of my uncle I was able to obtain data to work out the average figures between 1918 and 1926 of the income and expenses of

two estates in Strathdearn. I noted them as A. and B. in an article in the
Economic Journal.[21]

A. Balnespick consisted of 5300 acres of which 180 acres were arable,
100 acres had been planted and the remainder, 5020 acres, were moorland.

Income:	Rents from farms	£215
	Rents of shootings and fishings	£1000
		£1215

Expenditure:	Wages (keeper etc.), salary, insurances and repairs (almost entirely to farm steadings and permanent improvements) and miscellaneous	£751
	Rates, taxes, share of minister's stipend	£ 423
		£1174

Surplus: £41

The mansion house which was let with the shooting, and included in
the rent, required at least £1000 to be spent upon it to maintain the fabric
and bring it up to the tenants' requirements.

B. Clune consisted of 4727 acres of which 120 acres were arable, 126
acres were planted and 4481 acres were moorland.

Income:	Rents from farms	£192
	Rents of shootings and fishings	£1500
		£1692

Expenditure:	Wages (keeper etc.), salary, insurances and repairs (almost entirely to farm steadings and permanent improvements) and miscellaneous	£789
	Rates, taxes, share of minister's stipend	£657
		£1446

Surplus: £246

A new house had been completed since the war and had cost about
£10,000. It was let with the shooting and was included in the rent.

Up to the First World War and, even to a limited extent, up to the
second one, the way of life of a large section of the community – the
families of men in the army and navy, barristers, members of the Civil
Service of India and similar services, or in certain types of business – all
had fairly similar standards of living which only changed very gradually
from early Victorian times. In Strathdearn some owners spent their leave
on vacations in their homes there, the tenants of the other shootings were
generally not dissimilar.

The letting of shootings gave a certain amount of local employment. It has been calculated that, acre by acre, sheep farming and deer forests give much the same amount of employment and grouse moors a slightly greater proportion.[22] After the introduction of shooting driven grouse, there was a considerable amount of seasonal work. In driving grouse a line of beaters drives the grouse over a row of butts where the guns are concealed. By good fortune the harvest is so late in the Highlands that the temporary job of beating fits in well with the agricultural work of the year. About the early 1920s I know that the shooting tenant in Balnespick paid about £145 for two local lads to work as ghillies, for a man and a pony with panniers (£1 a day) and the beaters (6s.) a day with food. If the season were wet he would pay less.

Shooting rents are also of value to the community. I made some calculations for the period 1918-26 and found that the value of the sporting rights represented about two-thirds of the total rateable value of the parish, a good return from that part of the land (the moors) that had been almost valueless before the latter part of the eighteenth century.[23]

As an old woman one remembers small but not insignificant details. When I was a child, and my grandparents lived half the year at Balnespick, Grannie wore a cap, so did her sister-in-law, my great Aunt Janie, my other grandmother and ladies of that generation. It went with shawls and taking exercise by walking up and down the room and, of course, an afternoon drive when a ritual in the correct leaving of visiting cards made an object for the drive. (Visiting cards were, of course, always engraved. If one was in doubt about someone, one ran one's fingers over the words on the card to feel if the terrible solecism of printing them had been committed.) I can remember driving to Kyllachie for this purpose. The next generation, my mother and my aunt and their contemporaries, never wore caps or adopted many of these special mannerisms, but the afternoon drive lasted until the day when they ceased to be 'carriage company' and took to the purposeful motor car. By that time the leaving of cards was going out. Skirts reaching to the ground, and in more dressy outfits trailing on the ground at the back, were *de rigueur* until about the eighties and nineties when the more athletic ladies took to riding the bicycle. As a well-disciplined little girl I enjoyed watching the wobbly progress of my elders and betters, especially seeing a courtly male trying to doff his hat to greet a lady acquaintance. About the same time came country clothes, and tweed coats and skirts were worn when people came north. Girls could walk behind the guns for a day on the hill in skirts that only reached to their ankles or were even a bit shorter.

Of course, all through the period dressing for dinner was obligatory and even in the small house parties of two or three guests gentlemen armed the ladies into dinner. On Sundays we wore much more formal clothes than on week-days and, even in the country, we changed dresses to suit the occasion much more often. It was considered a great lapse of taste to be either over- or under-dressed (a point that some of the television shows rather miss).

I believe that so late as the 1830s people dined at 5.30pm and had tea in the evening. When I was young I used to stay with two old-fashioned families where, although dinner was at 7.30, an equipage of tea things was carried in about 9pm. In my mother's youth afternoon visitors might be offered a glass of wine and a slice of cake. I suppose that it was not until after the middle of the century that afternoon tea became a regular meal; in the country it was often eaten in the dining room. This lasted more or less till the Second World War. A great many households began the day well with family prayers before breakfast, a row of maids in their immaculate print dresses always being present. My father and grand-father were punctilious in not taking out the coachman and horses on Sunday. Meals were comparatively elaborate but there was much less variety in the dishes. At a house party, even for a small shoot, a six-course meal would be served, consisting of soup, fish, entrée, meat or game, sweet, savoury and dessert, but up till the First World War the coffee afterwards might be surprisingly bad. Ladies did not normally drink whisky. In the social circles I am writing of they did not smoke till 1910 or later. Port was a more usual drink than now and gin and cocktails did not come in till after the 1920s. From about the same time gentlemen were not entirely confined to the smoking room when they wanted to smoke a cigarette.

To maintain such a way of life, the staff of servants was standardized. It consisted of a cook, a house-maid and parlour-maid. These were often supplemented by kitchen-maid, under-house-maid or parlour-maid, lady's maid and, if there were children, nurse – they were never called nannies – and nursery-maid. Outdoor servants were basically coachman, gardener and keeper, often with a groom and other assistants added.

All, however, was not bliss and ease when people had staffs of domestics to wait on them. Servants had their weekly days off and the others did not normally do their work. They sometimes left at the most inconvenient moment or they did not get on with each other. Good ones, especially good cooks, were not easy to find and upon the cook depended the happiness of the entire household – employers and staff. Children had to mind their p's and q's with the cook. One only entered the kitchen on a message or at her invitation and received a portion of any delicacy that was going as a favour. When I think of the tutoring upon the proper use of a gun that the boys of a family received from the keeper, I feel sorry for the game, beasts and birds, of the present day, so apt to be the quarries of ill-trained sportsmen.

I think most people of my generation and the generations immediately following have grateful memories of all that they owe to beloved servants. I think of Mary, my Highland nurse. At the time when, as a child, I needed the support of a grown-up when I was ill or the world seemed strange to me, I remember how she sang to me, *Mo run geal dileas*, with a strange pentatonic twist to the air that seemed to come from immeasurably remoter times. Then there was Macrae, the keeper, true embodiment of the old family retainer. The proud possessor of my first car, I gave Macrae a lift from Inverness. My mother happened to be at the gate and he pulled out his watch, looked at it, and announced with misplaced pride that I was not five minutes behind 'the captain'. The captain was my brother. His reputation as a steady driver was not diminished, mine as a reckless speed merchant was established! Old servants, however, could be tyrannical to the more vulnerable members of the family or the staff.

Before the advent of the car we were dependent upon horses and our own feet. We walked a great deal. It was often easier to walk than to have a horse harnessed and then re-stabled and the harness cleaned. As a matter of course on Sundays we walked to the local kirk. On looking back what a lot of things one remembers that one saw when one was walking. Sunlight and shadow, birds or flowers, the scent of birch trees after rain. How many friendly meetings one had. A good many of the anecdotes that I have written down were collected in talk with people who happened 'to be going the same road' as myself. When riding, driving or motoring one did not store up the same wealth of impressions.

Social contacts were largely limited by the distance horses could cover. When we visited people at any distance our stay had to be prolonged until the horses had been fed and rested. And I can remember one or two occasions when we felt rather *de trop*. In the country most people had open carriages, wagonettes, brakes, gigs and pony traps. But we wrapped up well and we wore more and warmer clothing. In households such as ours the change from horses to a car came soon after 1900. At first, members of the family did not attempt to drive for the early cars were complicated and temperamental machines. They were also troublesome to look after with so much brass work and easily damaged paint. A chauffeur was employed and in our case the coachman was sent to learn to drive. He always hissed while he was cleaning the car as if he were grooming a horse and occasionally addressed it with a 'steady there now'. Ladies equipped themselves with motor veils tied over their hats for a drive in the car, which was almost always an open one with a 'cape-cart' type of hood. After the First World War most people learnt to drive their own cars. The first one was often given a pet name. Mine was called Williamina. Motor buses began to run twice daily between Inverness and Tomatin in the thirties and, as Lady Malkin noted with shrewd but kindly eyes, they 'brought the town into the country people's lives' and 'the girls began to wear silk stockings and pretty hats'.

To go back to memories of the long Victorian period – my parents and their family lived permanently in the country, but for us, like many more affluent friends who, because of their work or from choice, lived part of the time in London – we always referred to London as 'Town'. For people like us it was much more of a social centre than it is now. Every other year or so, my parents took rooms or rented a house for a month or two. This was the normal practice. We had many friends living in Belgravia, South Kensington or Chelsea and others came up for a time as, for instance, when a daughter was coming out or being presented. The houses had window-boxes full of flowers. Red carpets were constantly being laid. Until the 'weekend' became fashionable, church parade in the park was an occasion. For us, who lived in the north of Scotland with occasional long, night journeys by train to London, the rest of Britain was almost as remote as a foreign land.

Comparing the past with the present it is noteworthy how many more people try, in spite of penal taxation and death duties, to make their permanent home in the country instead of merely coming up for the shooting season. On the other hand shooting tenants do not bring up staff to settle in lodges for the season but make transient visits. Roads are made over the moors to convey urbanized tycoons up to the very butts where, once foot-free, the sportsmen strode over the moors. I hear there are further plans for the commercialisation of sport to enable deep-pursed visitors to indulge their blood lust, which make me feel sick.

Looking back on what one remembers, and what one has been told, of the Victorian period, I think that the salient feature was a feeling of security and of assurance that things were getting better and better, that God was indeed in His Heaven and that the work our empire builders were called on to do was helping to bring right to this world. At all levels of society people were largely free from the despicable vice of envy which besets the modern world.

The Village

About halfway along this bit of the road we come to Tomatin. It was probably moved from the other side of the river after Mitchell made his road and by the enterprise of the Macbeans of Tomatin. In the days before there was a direct railway connection between Inverness and the south, a great deal of traffic must have gone through it. Mr MacAskill has a tale that the daily coach between Inverness and Perth sometimes stopped at the shop, then owned by William Noble, a member of a family long settled in Strathdearn. One morning the shop was shut and Noble was still asleep. The guard put his horn close to the bedroom window and blew a blast. 'Wake up, wake up wifey!' cried Noble. 'Do you not hear the Last Trumpet?'

The village has developed with the times and, whereas most of our road has associations with the very uncomfortable past, at Tomatin one's thoughts are with the amenities of the present. The post office is a cell in a complicated ganglia of nerves that encircle the planet for the transmission of news and information. So late as 1834 the post office was at Inverness and the bright idea that the passing coach might leave the letters at Tomatin was being discussed. The house built for the district nurse is a token of the vast advance in medicine that is one of the least controversial benefits of the times we live in. There is no local tradition of curative herbs and whisky was regarded as a sovereign remedy.[24]

There was a long struggle led by Mary Mackintosh of Clune and Margaret Malkin of Corriebrough to get a district nurse appointed to Strathdearn; but her coming was not welcomed by everyone. I was told that some people said that there was little call for a woman from outside with all sorts of new-fangled ideas to be poking her nose into their houses. It happened, however, that very shortly after the first nurse arrived a man was badly hurt in an accident with a reaping machine. By her skilled assistance the nurse probably saved his life and her position in the community was assured. There have been several successive owners of the local shop, a country 'General Merchant' of the best kind with an amazing variety of wares from the utilitarian to the sophisticated – all of them with strong and diverse personalities – but the title 'Macdougall's Stores', almost as immutable as the Monadh Liath themselves, has remained above its windows.

The cluster of post-war council houses has been admirably sited, a little off the road. Close to them is a cottage, part of which is very old for it has been contrived out of an old carding mill. Such mills are rare in the Highlands. When I saw it, it had evidently been long out of use. A narrow bridge over a small burn led to the door. Presumably there had been a wheel to work the mill but it had disappeared. Inside there was a large cylinder covered with small metal spikes. As they revolved these could obviously disentangle and straighten the fibres of a fleece but how one got the wool on and off the cylinder I do not know. This mill was obviously one of the many attempts that were made to promote industries in the Highlands, such as a linen-spinning industry which flourished in Perthshire for a time in the eighteenth century and the series of projects for the stimulation of the fisheries from the seventeenth century onwards.

In Strathdearn people spun and knitted and wove their home-produced wool and, until well into the nineteenth century, were largely clad in their own handiwork. No export industry developed and, by the 1830s, they were beginning to buy their cloth. Weavers, of whom there had been seven, had disappeared long before my day. It is indeed a joy to think that at last there is once more a weaver in Strathdearn.

To make the wool cards for preparing the wool for spinning must have been a craftsman's job; and they must have been bought but possibly a skilled spinner, using the fine short fleece of the old breed of sheep, could have managed without them. Spinning was done on the spindle which was slow but enabled a woman to move about while spinning. Then, in the late eighteenth century, the muckle wheel was introduced. The wheel was turned by hand – first in one direction to twist the thread, then in the other to wind it on the spindle. I found a rather dilapidated muckle wheel in a disused house at the Coigs. The muckle wheel was quickly succeeded by the familiar types of spinning wheels – 'cocked up' or upright – which simultaneously spun and wound the yarn and are worked by a treadle.

By the 1940s spinning had become a rare accomplishment in Strathdearn and Mrs Macpherson at Croft Dhu was asked to go to Carrbridge to give a demonstration. But when I was young I remember that I rather took it for granted that our nearest neighbours, Annie Noble and her mother at Inverbrough, could spin. But even by that time crotal was almost the only vegetable dye that they used. It is a large, scaley lichen that grows on rocks. It gives a warm ruddy brown and is very easy to use as it needs no preparation or mordant. I have been told by women in the Islands that crotal 'that sees the sea' gives the best colour but Annie Noble poured scorn on such an idea and said that inland crotal was superior. Even the memory of the old skill in dyeing had almost disappeared.

Before the 1914 War it was fashionable to take an interest in Highland home industries – traditional industries carried on by the local people. The main object was to find a suitable market for them. It was work for which country ladies were well fitted and many of them worked hard at it. Someone came to stay with us who was interested in vegetable dyeing and most anxious to meet Annie Noble. When we called on her she was finishing a pair of homespun hose, as usual dyed with crotal but with a sickly purple band round the tops which I privately thought a disaster. (In those days hose-tops used to be knitted in very fancy stitches.) Our visitor's attention was at once riveted on the purple band and, in an awed voice, she asked what Annie had used to get that colour. 'Twink', replied Annie and produced a half-empty packet of a proprietory manufactured dye.

To go back to the carding mill. It is a late example of people's ingenuity in using the convenient supply of water-power that the many little burns running down the hillsides provided. In Strathdearn Mr Murdo MacAskill tells me he has discovered the remains of very small mills in streams conveniently near individual farms; thus the people of Strathdearn were saved a great deal of drudgery.

I was a little surprised that one did not come across querns, or even recollection of their use, in Strathdearn. In most districts in the West that I visited, people at least had heard of their use, and I met one woman who had actually used one. It was not difficult to obtain the actual querns – and, by the way, you cannot put an odd top stone on to an odd lower one, they were made to fit. A good quern can be turned with surprising ease.

There is no tradition or evidence in Strathdearn of the west coast and Island custom of fulling a finished web of cloth by soaking it in urine and then assembling the women of the neighbourhood to pummel and thump it to the accompaniment of appropriate songs. It is now spoken of as the *luadhadh*, anglicized into luath, and in folksy entertainment it is some-times re-enacted *without* the essential fluid. No doubt if the people of

Strathdearn had wished they could easily have fulled their cloth in their many hill streams.

A small and unpretentious corrugated-iron building where services are held on Sunday afternoons reminds me how formal, as well as gracious, Highland manners were in the old days. When Grannie and Grand-daddie went to church from Balnespick they walked, horses were not taken out on a Sunday, and anyone going their way fell in behind them and did not pass them.

Tomatin excels in one industry – the distilling of whisky. The origin of the making of *uisque beatha*, the water of life, goes back into the dimness of antiquity. It is a drink particularly acceptable in our rigorous Highland climate and, because of the particular quality of its water and good supply of peat, the Highlands have pre-eminent advantages in distilling it. Every contemporary local description, including those that I have quoted from, comments upon the large quantities that were drunk. According to the *Old Statistical Account* there were two inns and twelve public houses in the parish in 1793-4.[25] There was a great deal of local distilling beside the so useful little mountain burns and, until after the '45, the Act imposing a duty on spirits was not enforced. After that not only was the payment of duty enforced but the rate payable was raised by successive Acts. As a result there was a growing increase in illicit distilling and in the activities of the excisemen (known as gaugers because they had to gauge the amount of the malt in any liquor that they seized in order to assess the duty). A crisis point was reached in 1814 when an Act was passed prohibiting all distilling in the Highlands in stills of less than a 500-gallon capacity. Deep resentment was felt and there was so great an increase in illicit distilling that in 1823 a more lenient Act had to be passed and the provocation to break the law ceased.[26] The two stories I was told must be older than the 1814 Act. According to one tale local smugglers hid some illicitly distilled whisky in the pulpit of Dalarossie church. Mackintosh of Clune, my great-grandfather, heard of it and set out to investigate. Word of this reached the smugglers who sent the prettiest girl they could find to meet him on the way and delay him in pleasant conversation in order to give them time to remove the kegs of whisky.

The other story was said to relate to Freeburn Inn which replaced Dalmagarry in the 1820s but I rather suspect that it took place in the older building. A couple of gaugers seized some whisky. On their way to Inverness with the captured keg, to gauge the whisky and to lodge a prosecution, they stopped at an inn for some refreshment. For safety they appear to have taken the keg to an upper room. The owner of the still had followed them. He appealed to the maid-servant for help and asked her exactly where the gaugers had placed the keg. She told him it was against the wall. He asked her to go up to the room again on some excuse and to count the number of planks on each side of the keg. She did so and, from the room below, he counted the boards in the ceiling, bored a hole through the one on which the keg was standing, and so through the bottom of the keg. Of course the whisky all drained away and the gaugers were left with an empty keg and no grounds for prosecution.

Macbean of Tomatin bought the neighbouring land of Free and started a distillery there. This was, unfortunately, a failure but the quality of the local water there is superlative for distilling a type of whisky particularly suitable for blending and the company that succeeded him has built up one of the finest distilleries in the Highlands and therefore in Scotland and in the world.

The other example of modern enterprise, Freeburn Hotel, is rather further down the road but still on the Tomatin estate. It was during the ownership of the Macbeans that it replaced Dalmagarry Inn and in my young days it was still called the Freeburn Inn. I can remember the superlative country fare from the home farm that one feasted on there.

6

Where All the Roads Meet

On a side road, just beyond the shop, a flat stone used to be pointed out to me and I was told that Bonnie Prince Charlie breakfasted on it. The record of his travels has, however, been carefully recorded and it is rather difficult to see when this happened.

A little further on, moreover, there are associations with a yet remoter past. Down by the river a slab of stone was found that bore traces of the handiwork of the people who lived in Strathdearn at the period when the Highlands were becoming dimly known to history. A plough happened to knock against this stone when the field by the river was being ploughed and so it was dug up. Fortunately, it was a member of the Dunbar family, with his love of history, who was ploughing. He noticed that there were carvings upon the stone and so he did not break it up but laid it on the edge of the field. I came over to see it and, although it must be nearly fifty years ago, I can still remember the thrill I felt when I recognized two of the well-known Pictish symbols, the Crescent and the Broken Rod. The stone was carefully preserved and is now in the Scottish Museum of Antiquities. It always seems rather a reproach to Scots archaeologists that they have failed to solve the problem of the meaning of the Pictish symbols. The position of this stone, down by a turbulent river and in the middle of a forest infested by wolves and other animals, makes it unlikely that it was a tomb stone. It was, however, on an important track. Surely it is a plausible theory that the symbols were like the characters in Chinese writing which represent words and not letters, and that here the carvings represent a notice of the boundaries of the territories of a tribe or a magnate or of someone's territorial rights, probably hunting or pasturage. Of course, similar symbols, like these inscriptions, would be put on the tomb of the chief or magnate. I venture such suggestions after seeing a Pictish symbol stone in its regional setting.

Stone with Pictish Symbols found at Invereen, 1932. National Museum of Antiquities of Scotland.

In so many cases the use of the land round them has changed, but I wonder if any work has been done in considering them from this angle.

Rather further back, by the road itself, there is a line of dilapidated trees. I was once told that at Hallowe'en a figure 'with a face like the bark of a tree' and dressed in skins would rush out from behind one of them and belabour any unwary passerby with his club. I know of no similar tale in Gaelic tradition but it is very like some incidents in the Norse Sagas, and I have heard that in South Uist which, of course, was overrun by the Norsemen, a recognized Hallowe'en prank was to dress up in skins and pretend to attack people. The Norsemen never succeeded in getting a permanent foothold in Moray although there is a tale of a Norse princess and a stone commemorating her below the Streens. But the Norsemen did not live in entirely isolated barbarism and I wonder if this is not something that they shared with older races.

The actual road was made by Mitchell but Mr MacAskill has noted the many old tracks about here. They were tracks to various farms used before the road was made. Their courses are mainly dictated by the lie of the land, such as boggy patches and hillocks, and these existed long before man first found his way to Strathdearn. Man himself has been here a long, long time, living in hut circles on each side of the river, burying his dead on a fertile shelf of the hillside, setting up a stone with his symbols close to where, centuries later, Wade was to construct his military road. Moreover, just across the river, there is the Fairy Hill, a place name that commemorates ancient stories, told by a long-ago people about a race more ancient than their own, garbled, exaggerated and changed in the constant retelling. One wonders if the tale of this strange visitant was the fag-end of a story once known throughout north-western Europe or if it is the memory of an actual survivor from a superseded civilization, a displaced 'aborigine' lurking on the outskirts of the territory from which his people had been displaced.

All this is of course fanciful thinking. There is another much better known and authenticated local story that I am tempted to treat in the same way. It is located close to the pass known as Stairsneach nan Gaidheal, 'the Threshold of the Highlands', through which Wade's road passes into Strath Nairn from Strathdearn. The *New Statistical Account* describes it as 'a green spot called *Uaigh an duine-bheo*, the living man's grave'.[1] The story is that Mackintosh and Macgillivray of Dunmaglass disagreed about the march between their lands. Macgillivray offered to find a man who would declare upon oath that he was standing on

Macgillivray's land and would agree to the penalty that, if he were found to be swearing falsely, he would be buried alive. Accordingly the man was produced and he swore by the head under his bonnet that earth under his feet belonged to Dunmaglass. He was, however, searched and it was found that his shoes had been partly filled with earth from Macgillivray's land and that, under his bonnet, he had put a cock's head. So he was buried alive. There are points to note about this story. Firstly, the story is not as old as one would expect for such a barbarous tale. Macgillivray, though he had been in Dunmaglass for some time, only got a feu of it from Campbell of Cawdor in 1626.[2] The Macgillivrays were members of Clan Chattan and always close and loyal supporters of Mackintosh who was chief of Clan Chattan. There are other cases when old stories are re-dated to fit into later and more familiar facts, such as the tale about the Earl of Mar. I think that there is a feel of something very ancient and primitive about this story, not quite in character with the kind of society it is ascribed to. Secondly, in the old days, Highlanders had little regard for human life but I know of no other case in the Highlands of a man being buried alive. On the other hand it was certainly done by the ancient Celts. In Denmark, in the peat, the bodies of some of the victims were discovered and are preserved in a museum where I took good care *not* to see them when I visited Copenhagen. I have been told of sacrificial pits in Gaul. Moreover, the place is a natural line of demarcation between two straths and that would be quickly obvious to primitive people.

Travellers on the Road

We have now come to about the middle of the Strath. The river turns eastwards. Mitchell's stretch of the road unites with the older Wade's road and, for some distance, obliterates it. The railway follows a parallel course and now the new road takes a similar line. One feels certain that this was the old, old way people took in crossing the Strath long before the first road was thought of. The stone with Pictish symbols was found close to Wade's road just before it reached this point and I feel that surely it was a sign post or notice board (if one may apply such terms to a stone slab) set up beside a well-known track.

By historical times one can begin to picture some of the folk who came this way. In the first place there would be pedestrians coming from surprising distances. The Highlanders were great walkers and went, indeed, over hill as well as dale. Sir Aeneas in his *Notes*, quotes an astounding example. In the past, Mackintosh of Mackintosh had employed 'running footmen', part of whose duty was to deliver messages. One of them, *in one day*, starting very early in the morning and returning late at night, would deliver a message at Invercauld. Invercauld is close to Braemar. The distance 'as the crow flies', i.e. in an absolutely straight line, is about thirty miles, but the messenger, after following Wade's road through the Slochd, would have to find his way across Strath Spey with its formidable river, and by one of the passes over the vast bulk of the Cairngorms.[3] 'Colonel Anne', well-known for her part in the '45, was the daughter of Farquharson of Invercauld, which indicates a date for this story. This was an unusual exploit but, even as late as the beginning of the nineteenth century, it was not unusual for people to walk to and from Inverness with their market produce. (Inverness is about twelve miles from Moy and considerably further from the top of the Strath.)

What people could not carry was conveyed on pack-horses – or rather ponies – in two creels hung on a wooden pack-saddle. When I was in the Western Islands collecting for the museum one could still see the peats being carried from the moss in this way. Wheeled transport was, however, taking over so that I was able to rescue several of the wooden pack-saddles. A wooden hook was carved on each side onto which the panniers were hung. Because wood was scarce in the islands, the saddles were made of several bits of wood, nailed together. I was, however, given a very much older pack-saddle from Perthshire of exactly the same shape but carved out of one piece of timber. In the old days, part of the rental due by a tenant consisted of a given number of 'carriages', i.e. the service of a pack-horse and a man to convey a load of peat, corn or whatever to a destination.

By the thirteenth century some cattle were being sent from the Highlands to Lowland markets. The Scots export trade to the Continent consisted of wool, which would come from the Lowlands, and skins and hides. Inverness was one of the eight burghs exporting these to France, the Baltic and especially to Campveere in the Netherlands. It was a growing trade. Hides, of course, were the skins of cattle; skins were of 'daes and raes' = red deer and roe deer as well as 'weathers', 'conies', otters and martins.[4] It was a very old trade. In the Museum of Antiquities in Edinburgh there is a tiny clay model of a bale of hides, apparently a charm or votive offering that was found in a broch. One can well picture how the furs contained in such bales would be collected from the mountain glens, bundled together and carried by this convenient route to Inverness. (After the Union of the Crowns the droving of the cattle became important but Inverness was only on a drove route of secondary importance.)

Inverness, as a Royal Burgh, was privileged to carry on foreign trade and received imports as well as goods for export. With the wares from the fairs at these burghs, pack-men travelled the country. They were adventurous. One only comes across allusions to them when they had got into trouble, but I have read of instances of their presence in the islands and the far west, so I am sure that the pack-men took their way across Strathdearn. The pack-men did more than sell their wares. It was they who carried a knowledge of the great oral heritage of Gaelic epics to the remotest parts of the Highlands. We are also indebted to them as the collectors from whom Finlay MacNab of Bovain gathered many of the poems in his great collection, the *Duanaire*, which James MacGregor, Dean of Lismore, completed and presented it to MacCailéin Mór, the Earl of Argyll. *The Book of the Dean of Lismore* is of course one of the most precious source books for a study (and appreciation) of our poetry and stories. In a poem addressed to a friend, Finlay MacNab urges him to collect more poems from the strolling pack-men and poets.

1. As to the Song-book of the Pillagers, should you be pleased to write it, I myself have got from the pack-man somewhat that may go to fill it.
2. Though many are the evil men who are set on spoiling the folk, not one thing in the world is got from them in return for it.
3. It is a custom of the strollers, though they should have but a mile to go, that they will not reach until nightfall the house which they make their tryst.
4. I shall not name their ancestry, I have naught of their story, save their being in the evening with the dogs in their train.
5. Thou Dugall, my comrade, son of John of polished blades, thou who hast the guidance of the strollers, do thou write the Song-book.
6. Write expertly, learnedly, their lore and their tuneful works; bring unto MacCailéin no poem lacking artistry to be read.[5]

The cairds must have taken the same road as the pack-men. They were versatile craftsmen. They could mould horn spoons. The tinkers, who are their descendants, remember that they, themselves, once had this skill but I never could persuade any of them to practise it. The cairds, with their portable equipment, could make a brooch out of a silver coin. Sometimes one can see the initial engraving of the coin on the underside. They, of course, could do small metal repairs. I have seen a contraption for weighing wool, partly made out of an old dirk, that was probably their work. They would carve the wooden pommels of dirks and ornament them with interlaced patterns. But I never discovered how much they specialized in the different branches of their activities. In my youth, passing tinkers generally camped in the wood at Soilshan at a place more conveniently placed near Wade's road than the later branch road by Mitchell. As the ancient track taken by cairds evidently followed much the same line as Wade's road one wonders if this was a traditional camping site.

Very different was the appearance of a chief, accompanied by his 'tail', and on the way to meet another great man or, perhaps less happily for himself, to obey a summons from the authorities in Inverness. Sir Aeneas Mackintosh gives a list of the attendants that accompanied a chief in the old days. Firstly, he had a Standard Bearer. Sir Aeneas still retained one in his service. Secondly, a chief was attended by a gentleman of the Name who acted as a companion to his lord, delivered messages, wrote letters and gave orders. Thirdly, the chief used to have a Bard or Poet, well acquainted with the genealogy of all the families of the Name and able to compose and sing verse in praise of the gallant actions of the chief's predecessors. By Sir Aeneas's time (end of eighteenth century) the services of this attendant had long been dispensed with. Fourthly, he had a Piper, 'a man of such consequence that he had a Boy attending to carry his pipe, when he did not play'. His pipes were decorated with ribbons of the colours of the livery of the family. Sir Aeneas's piper was a MacCrimmon trained in Skye. Fifthly, in the old days, the chief was preceded by several 'running footmen' dressed in white linen with sashes of the colour of the family livery.[6]

Sir Walter Scott, in writing *Waverley*, has transmitted to us a record of his intimate knowledge of life in the Highlands. Evan, Vick Ian Vohr's faithful foster brother, proudly tells Edward Waverley of the chief's 'tail'. Edward expresses surprise. Evan tells him that it is with all his usual followers when he visits those of the same rank'.

Firstly there is his *hanchman*, or right-hand man; then his bard or poet;

then his *bladier* or orator, to make harangues to the great folks whom he visits; then his *gillymore* or armour-bearer, to carry his sword and target and his gun; then his *gillycasfliuch* who carries him on his back through the sikes [bogs] and brooks; then his *gillycomstrian*, to lead his horse by the bridle in steep and difficult paths; then his *gillytrush-harnish*, to carry his knapsack; and the piper and the piper's man and it may be a dozen young lads beside, that have no business but are just 'boys of the belt' to follow the laird and do his honour's bidding.

The Lords of the Isles fostered the classical forms of Gaelic art. Poets were then the honoured guests of high and low throughout the Western Highlands and Islands. Clan Ranald continued to support the MacMhuirichs, the family bards of the Lords of the Isles and, as late as the seventeenth century, Macleod of Macleod and Macleod of Bernera were regularly entertaining bands of poets – as one of them gleefully recalled. They found other patrons in Argyll and Perthshire. One has a feeling that the clans of the North East who so steadily opposed the Lords of the Isles, would not be so appreciative of this culture. Mackintosh's attitude politically was ambivalent, because he held land of the Lord of the Isles in Lochaber, but surely a poet or two took their way through Strathdearn.

In recalling these peaceful comings and goings across the Strath, one has to remember that, in the old days, there was an ever-present menace of violence. As the saying went 'a man's hand had to keep his head'. The well-being or very existence of a clan depended upon the ability of its clansmen to defend it. In time of need the fighting men of a clan were summoned by 'the fiery cross', a stick with one end burnt and the other dipped in blood, to signify the fate of those who disobeyed and of their homes. When the clan was summoned by the fiery cross in the Rising of the '15, within nine hours the cross was carried thirty-two miles and 5000 men rose. One must picture the passing, time and again, of the messenger summoning the clansmen of the very warlike Clan Mackintosh to fight for their king – as, from Bannockburn onwards they did in many of his tussles with the 'auld enemy' and against his insurgent nobles, or in support of their Chief in the long drawn-out feuds with some of his neighbours.

To pass from war to peace, weddings were great occasions in the Highlands. I have quoted from a contemporary account of a wedding at Dalarossie. Many similar parties must have come along this road on their way to the church at Moy. But sometimes, especially in the case of the marriage of an heir or heiress, which was usually a matter of careful arrangement, the home-bringing of the bride involved a journey. For instance, in 1717, there was a grand wedding between the son of Fraser of Lovat and the Laird of Grant's daughter. The wedding was, no doubt, at Freuchie (the old name of Castle Grant) and a number of the bridegroom's relatives and friends bore him company when he went there. No doubt they came and went by way of the Stairsneach nan Gaidheal and the Slochd. On their way back they sang:

> We will go home, come away home,
> We will go home to the Aird,
> Leave we the Grants of the porridge,
> We are the Frasers of the Kail.[7]

Funerals were more important functions than weddings. Highlanders had a great desire to be laid to rest in the burial place of the family. The dead were sometimes carried great distances. I have been told that relays of bearers would be ready to take each other's place. When the whole procession did stop for a rest, it was the custom in some districts for everyone to place a stone on a cairn. I have seen groups of these cairns on the road along Loch Eil. There are traditions of such cairns in Strathdearn, but I have never noticed any although many funeral parties must have passed this way.

The burial of a chief was a really great affair. Sir Aeneas gives a description of what happened at the zenith of the armed power of the clans. The first duty of the chief's heir was to send out invitations to all his relatives and neighbours. It was obligatory upon the clansmen to attend, fully armed, and any other chiefs who had been invited to be present at the funeral were also escorted by their armed clansmen. Sir Aeneas noted: 'Strict precedence was observed to avoid which might lead to bloodshed which nearly happened in 1727' (A.M. Mackintosh gives the date as 1731) at the funeral of Lachlan, the twentieth Laird.

The presence of large, armed followings of both the host and his guests was a valuable opportunity to demonstrate the fighting strength of the clans, besides being a mark of respect to the deceased. One senses the very real pride of race in the accounts of funerals in the writings of Master James Fraser, author of *Chronicles of the Frasers* (written in the seventeenth century). He was evidently a connoisseur of funerals and took a loyal pride in those of deceased chiefs of Clan Fraser. Such terms as 'a most glorious funeral' and 'sumptuous and solemn' are among his comments.

He was critical of chiefs who did not bring a suitable retinue to the interment of their neighbours. He wondered at Mackenzie of Seaforth, who makes no figure at any kind of burial.[8]

Such elaborate funerals can only have taken place when the clans had grown large and their organization had developed. The burial place of the Chiefs of Mackintosh is at Petty. In earlier times it was in Inverness. (Until the sixteenth century they styled themselves 'of Connage' – a site near Petty and the Moray Firth. After 1502 they took the style of 'of Dunachton' – in Strath Spey. The term 'of', of course, denoted their main place of residence.) If the funeral took place from Connage, small groups of relatives and retainers of Mackintosh and those of the other members of Clan Chattan, that confederation of clans, would make their way from Strathdearn and Strath Spey to attend the funeral of their Chief. By the time Mackintosh acquired Dunachton, the Mackintoshes and some other members of Clan Chattan, notably the Macphersons, had developed into considerable communities. If a Chief died in Strath Spey, a long, long procession would have wended its way across Strathdearn. Sir Aeneas, recalling traditions of the old days, said that the piper attended with a black flag tied to his pipes, the 'hearse having six cross bars' was carried on the bearers' shoulders, 'and old women accompanying the procession, sang a melancholy song, lamenting the deceased – this was called the "Coronich".'

After Dunachton was burnt down by Keppoch in 1689 Mackintosh acquired Dalcross Castle, and a particularly magnificent funeral, costing £700 and attended by 2000 mourners, was held there. I do not know what happened after the murder of Lachlan (14th Chief) in 1524, while hunting in Strathdearn, or if Malcolm (10th Chief), who apparently lived at Moy in his old age, actually died there. But Moy was apparently considered inconveniently remote in 1731 when Lachlan (20th Chief) died in the house he had built on the shore of Loch Moy, for his body was taken to Dalcross Castle where it lay in state for two months until his successor could arrive; he received a funeral almost as grand as that of his father.

That was the last of the great funerals with a display of armed force. Mackintosh finances had been embarrassed by too great a display and the style of living was reduced. The next Chief died and was buried in Edinburgh and, after that, the Act abolishing Hereditary Jurisdiction, and the repressive legislation that followed the '45, rendered elaborate funerals impossible. After the '45 the family of Mackintosh of Mackintosh made their permanent home at Moy. Widely respected as they are, the funerals of Chiefs have been attended by great concourses of mourners from the surrounding districts. The outward appearance of these funerals has altered but there is continuity with the past in some of the sounds. The heart-breaking notes of the 'Lament' and the slow tramp of the multitude of feet link us with the past and also are a sign and symbol that loyalty to a Chief and pride in a name still survive.

This central point where so many tracks and roads cross each other, and where people of such diverse kinds must have taken their way on such different errands, saw the penultimate event in that most tragic and decisive crisis in Highland history, the march north of the main Jacobite army in 1746 and its retreat after Culloden. But this road was the scene of earlier phases of the struggle and the story of it is better told later.

7

Moy and Clan Mackintosh

The Nucleus of the Clan

A little further on, our road comes to a part known locally as 'the Bends' where, for about a mile and a half, it runs along the shores of Loch Moy. The attention of the driver and even of his passengers was here concentrated upon what was likely to appear round a series of blind corners. It is when one is old and one mentally revisits the road that, from the sparse data available, one has leisure to try to build up a story of the past.

At about this point Wade's military road finally parts company with the diversion constructed by the Parliamentary Commission. It leads towards the Threshold of the Highlands (Stairsneach nan Gaidheal) and crosses the Nairn about a mile further up.

Again and again, in following the road across Strathdearn, there have been associations with Clan Mackintosh. The home of the Chief of the clan is close to the loch, and the land the road runs through forms the setting for some of the most vivid traditional stories about the clan. The history of Clan Mackintosh is both complicated and eventful but, to put these incidents in their historical context, one can distinguish five periods. They overlap to some extent but they are – a. The founder's family development into the nucleus of a clan; b. Its struggle for existence during the dominance of the Comyns; c. Two major feuds and Mackintosh's relations with his feudal superiors; d. Mackintosh's involvement in the Jacobite cause; e. Mackintosh at Moy Hall.

As already stated, Shaw, a younger son of the third Earl of Fife, had been in the army with which Malcolm IV subdued a revolt in Moray. The King 'planted' the province with his loyal supporters and, in 1163, Shaw received a grant of Petty, in the fertile Laich of Moray, and of the

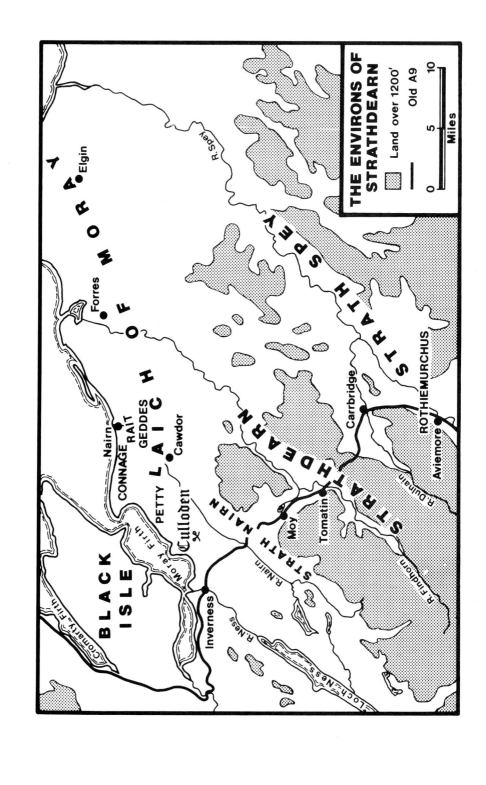

THE ENVIRONS OF
STRATHDEARN

Land over 1200'

Old A9

0   5   10
Miles

Elgin

MORAY

Forres

Nairn

BLACK
ISLE

LAICH OF MORAY

CONNAGE
RAIT
GEDDES
Cawdor
PETTY
Culloden

Cromarty Firth

Moray Firth

Inverness

R. Ness

Loch Ness

STRATH NAIRN

R. Nairn

Moy

Tomatin

STRATHDEARN

Carrbridge

R. Findhorn

R. Dulnain

STRATH SPEY

R. Spey

ROTHIEMURCHUS

Aviemore

Forest of Strathdearn.[1] If this grant were more than a verbal one, no copy or record survives.

Uncertainty about the terms of tenure of their most valuable land was to be the bugbear of the Mackintoshes for generations. So far as Petty is concerned, it was the considered opinion of the learned and painstaking historian of his clan, the late A.M. Mackintosh, that the Mackintoshes were no more than 'kindly tenants', i.e. tenants so well established on their holdings that the proprietor was under a generally recognized obligation not to remove them.[2] So far as the Forest of Strathdearn was concerned it became more definite.

Above the royal grant to Shaw there was a wider grant of land to the Bishops of Moray — these layers of rights to ownership are a feature of the history of the times — and until 1336 the Bishop is said to have reserved the Island in Loch Moy as a holiday retreat for himself. One can imagine his arrival upon a brief interlude from the cares of his diocese. These were no light burdens for the temporal powers of the Scots bishops were very great and many of them nobly played their part in the War of Independence. Of course, the great man would have dispensed with most of his usual entourage but one can imagine the figures of the small group, clear cut and angular like the figures in the illumination of a contemporary MS. There would be a bodyguard of some sort, a chaplain, a scrivener to take down any messages or orders in the beautiful script of the twelfth century. There would be verderers with hawks and hounds and a few members of his domestic household much concerned about all the paraphernalia of their various offices. They would all come up the narrow path through the Streens, as the most direct route from Elgin, wend their way through the broken ground and be ferried across the Loch to the island. In 1336 the Bishop of Moray granted the Barony of Moy to William, later 7th Chief, and after the Reformation it was held of the King.

Shaw and his descendants adopted the patronym of Mac-an-Tóisich = Mackintosh — and for five generations they followed much the same pattern of life. They all actively served the Crown. Shaw, himself, was made the Keeper of the Royal Castle at Inverness — the *Caput Capitanus* was an important official in the organization of Sheriffdoms that the active, efficient line of kings who were the direct lineal descendants of Malcolm Canmore, was building up. This office of Keeper of Inverness Castle was hereditary in Shaw's family for some generations. Then it was lost during the calamitous period that was to follow, then regained and lost once more.

Besides Shaw, other members of the family played their part in serving the King in war and in administrative work. They also were adding to their land. Shaw's grandson, before he succeeded as head of the family in 1240, obtained Geddes and Rait not far from Petty. The form of tenure is not stated but it seems to have been more definite than the right to Petty. He also, in 1236, got a lease of Rothiemurchus, in the upper valley of the Spey, from the Bishop of Moray. Members of the family must constantly have crossed the Strath on their way from one of their possessions to the other and, of course, they would have enjoyed hunting in the forest. One can trace a fanciful parallel between these early Mackintoshes, returning from fighting the King's enemies and rebels or administering some newly formed area of government, hunting the red deer or, with luck, killing a predatory wolf or two or even a wild boar in the forest on the one hand, and six hundred years later, officers returning on leave from foreign service and, with flintlocks and muzzle-loaders, shooting the grouse on the surrounding moors on the other.

Shaw and his immediate descendants were living in a period of fundamental changes. The ancient Scots kingdom of Alba was becoming divided into the Lowlands and the Highlands. The feudal system was being introduced. Norwegian claims to sovereignty over part of the Western Isles were finally extinguished. Within the Highlands a new form of social organization was developing which affected the family founded by Shaw. Similar families of the more fortunately placed and abler men tended to stick together and to acquire adherents. They were becoming the nuclei from which the oldest of the Highland clans were developing. Shaw's descendants, the Mackintoshes, received the allegiance of Gillivray, the ancestor of the Macgillivrays, and of Bean, the ancestor of the Macbeans, at a time when help was very needful for their survival.

At almost the end of the thirteenth century the story of the Mackintoshes changed course. Ferquhard, great-great-grandson of Shaw, had been appointed, or chosen, to lead the men of Badenoch in Alexander III's defence against the invasion of Hakon, King of Norway. After the repulse of the Norwegians he stayed with Alexander, Lord of Islay, and romance suddenly appeared in the bare narratives of the early Mackintoshes. One fancies that high-born girls of marriageable age were well chaperoned as useful bargaining counters in the web of family alliances but, as A.M. Mackintosh discreetly puts it, 'The intercourse of the young couple was at first of an unauthorised character,' and, this being discovered, Ferquhard fled – one longs to know how Mora handled the situation. In any case all was forgiven. Ferquhard returned and was duly married. Shortly afterwards he was killed in a quarrel and Alexander of Islay, his brother-in-law (his wife's brother), brought up Angus, his infant son and, in due course, arranged a most advantageous marriage for him. This was with Eva, the daughter and heiress of Dougal Dall, descendant of Gillichattan Mor, the Chief of Clan Chattan. By this marriage Angus received Eva's inheritance of Glenloy and Loch Arkaig in Lochaber. He was also accepted as the Chief of Clan Chattan. Clan Chattan, in the words of a Mackintosh historian, 'consisted of various families and septs, bearing diverse names who had banded themselves together for the purpose of defence'.[3]

Angus and Eva lived for a time in Lochaber. (To avoid misunderstanding of what eventually happened, it may be pointed out that Lochaber did not belong to the Lord of Islay and only came into the possession of his family later on. He must have used his influence which, as one of the three most powerful men in the western Highlands, was very great, to arrange the marriage.) I have travelled far in space and time from recollections of the road along Loch Moy but Eva's marriage to Angus was to have consequences that were to affect Clan Mackintosh and the people who passed this way for hundreds of years.

The Struggle for Survival

One can assume that, during Ferquhard's adventures and the minority of his son, the rest of his relations and their adherents went on living on their other lands in the Laich of Moray and Rothiemurchus, and retained their interest in the Forest of Strathdearn. Unfortunately for them the times were most difficult. After the choice of John Balliol as King of the Scots at Berwick in 1292, events quickly moved towards the outbreak of the first War of Independence. More immediately affecting the group of Mackintosh kinsfolk was the rise of the great Comyn family, then reaching the zenith of its power. Comyns had been the efficient servants of the Scots Kings since the eleventh century and they had reaped a rich reward.

According to the *Scots Peerage* the family was perhaps the most powerful in Scotland at that time and 'by marriage or inheritance members of it included three earls and thirty two knights'.[4] Among the lesser offices of this great family, those which particularly affected the Mackintoshes, was that of Keeper of the Royal Castle of Inverness (once held by a member of their own family), the Lordship of Lochaber (where Angus and his wife had their home) and the Lordship of Badenoch bordering on Rothiemurchus.

Comyns also occupied the most valuable holdings that Shaw and his successors had acquired, the lands of Petty, Connage, Geddes and Rait in the fertile Laich of Moray; all that remained to the Mackintoshes were the bleak birch woods of Strathdearn and the sombre pine forests of Rothiemurchus. As Sir Aeneas seems to assume, when he mentioned the remains of foundations of small houses on the island in Loch Moy, it was a refuge in this period, like the artificial lake dwellings that existed in primitive times in Britain and other parts of Western Europe, and which as 'crannocks' (crannogs) are mentioned as existing in the Highlands in writings of the sixteenth century. The Mackintosh's life must have resembled that of the backwoodsmen of America, the kind of life in which members of the clan, centuries later, were to show a hardy ability to prosper.

Remote as Strathdearn then was, news of great events must have filtered through to it – the invasion of Scotland in 1296 – Sir Andrew of Moray's campaign in the North, his brilliant victory, with Wallace as co-adjutor at Stirling Bridge, and his unfortunate death. After Wallace's defeat at Falkirk in 1298 the defence of Scotland depended upon the Comyn leaders, especially upon John Comyn, Lord of Badenoch (related to the Earl of Buchan, who had been the Guardian of Scotland), with whom for a short time Robert the Bruce was associated. Eventually, Edward I invaded Scotland in force and penetrated as far north as Morayshire (in 1303). It is a tribute to the Mackintosh clan that it is taken for granted that no collaboration was even hinted at between the deeply wronged Mackintosh family and the powerful invader who was also the enemy of their supplanters. The sacrilegious murder of the Red Comyn, the Lord of Badenoch, by Robert the Bruce in 1306, was a turning point in Scots history but, though it must have pleased them, it brought no immediate relief to the Mackintosh family. Fresh trouble arose in 1308 when Angus and Eva were obliged to leave her lands in Lochaber and return to Rothiemurchus. This, in the history books, is ascribed to the enmity of Angus Og. Angus Og of Islay and Angus Mackintosh were, however, on the same side and were to be companions-in-arms at Bannockburn. Lochaber, moreover, did not belong to Angus Og then, but to a Comyn, and was only granted to him by Bruce after the forfeiture of the Comyns. It is surely obvious that the official who administered the Comyn Lordship of Lochaber learned from his colleague in Moray or Badenoch that the Mackintoshes were *persona non grata* and took steps to get rid of them.

By 1309, however, the family fortunes were definitely on the mend. Bruce, as his strength grew, was freeing the country and he led a formidable campaign against the Earl of Buchan, the chief centre of Comyn power in the North-east. After routing the enemy at Inverurie his forces harried Buchan. Two years later he led a devastating raid into England and Angus was among his followers. At the Battle of Bannockburn, Angus again led a contingent of his kinsfolk and adherents, whom we can now term his clan. In 1319 Randolph, Earl of Moray, Bruce's nephew, granted him the lands of Benchar in Badenoch. Although the extent of the land included in the grant is not stated, it must have been extensive because all the original members of Clan Chattan, who had apparently remained in Lochaber, now came to settle in Badenoch while members of Clan Cameron took the chance of occupying the land that they had vacated. Unfortunately this transference set the scene for two constantly recurring sources of trouble for the future chiefs of Clan Mackintosh – the Macpherson claim to the chiefship of Clan Chattan and the dispute with the Camerons over the ownership of the Lochabar lands.

Angus was succeeded by William, who evidently had a strong appreciation of the value of property. In 1336 he obtained a grant of the Barony of Moy from the Bishop of Moray and also, a year later, a lease of Rothiemurchus, apparently for an unspecified period. He also endeavoured to regain occupation of his grandmother, Eva's, lands in Lochaber. So fixed was his desire to repossess them that he directed in his Will that, after the funeral ceremony at Connage, his body should be taken to an island in Loch Arkaig in Lochaber and buried there. The apparent obsession of successive Chiefs of Mackintosh to get occupation of land in Lochaber, and the resulting feuds with the Camerons and the Macdonalds of Keppoch, persisted for hundreds of years and, directly and indirectly, was to have its effects on the people of Strathdearn.

Although the Mackintoshes had considerably recovered their position they had still not regained a good deal of what they had lost during the

Comyn domination. No member of the family had been appointed Keeper of Inverness Castle and, although William had obviously resumed occupation of Connage, the lands of Geddes and Rait, equally or more valuable, for which the Mackintoshes had obtained a better title, were still in the hands of a branch of the Comyns whom they clearly did not feel strong enough to tackle.

Hostilities with the Camerons, however, continued and the latter, in 1370, raided Badenoch. Mackintosh collected all the forces he could and hurried after them in pursuit. He came up with them at Invernahavon, a spot a little to the west of modern Kingussie. In the battle that followed, there was evidence of the rivalry within Clan Chattan that was to develop into a constant source of trouble in the history of the Chiefs of Mackintosh. The Macphersons and the Davidsons, both members of Clan Chattan, claimed the honour of fighting on the right in the battle line. Mackintosh gave the right to the Davidsons. The Macphersons then refused to take part in the fight. But when the Mackintoshes were getting the worst of it, they came to their assistance and, later on, the Macphersons claimed that they were the rightful Chiefs of Clan Chattan. In the Mackintosh history, and also that of the Macphersons, tedious page after tedious page records the arguments, the meetings, the appeals for arbitration that cropped up again and again and again. The dispute with the Camerons continued.

The learned and painstaking historian of the Clan Mackintosh (to me a merry and charming little old cousin), is at great pains to identify Clan Cai and Clan Qwhewyl, who were the opponents in the famous combat on the Inches at Perth in 1396, with Clan Chattan and Clan Cameron respectively. Cameron histories agree that this identification is probably correct.[5] The combat took place in specially prepared lists on the North Inch of Perth before the King, the Queen, the Court and a large audience. It was a fight to the death between sides of probably thirty (the accounts vary) champions armed with swords and targes.[6]

To me, this organized fight to the death of men before the King (Robert III), his Queen and his court seems to be a shocking example of the barbarity of the Lowlands in those times. The alleged reason was that the warfare between two 'tribes' unsettled a whole district – but this is a poor excuse. Before the coming of the road and the railway, Badenoch and Lochaber were pleasantly remote from Lowland concern and both the Mackintoshes and the Camerons were only beginning to develop into the formidable clans that they eventually became. It was an age when people enjoyed sanguinary entertainments – tournaments, bear and bull baitings, public executions. One is glad that this form of entertainment was not repeated.

This contest has no connection with our road, but one could hardly write about the Mackintoshes without mentioning it and it had one permanent result. Because Lachlan, the Chief, was too old to take part in the combat on the Inches, the clan was led by his cousin Shaw and, in reward, Lachlan transferred to him the lease of Rothiemurchus in 1396. The feud with the Camerons was quiescent for a time and the Mackintoshes probably gained self-confidence to tackle their other enemy.

The power of the Comyns had been greatly eroded. Other families were rising to power at their expense and there are several local traditions in which they figure as the bad guys who are deservedly done down. There is a fine, but wholly mythical, Grant one, and I and my brothers, as children, fervently believed in the saying that, 'While there are leaves in the forest, there is guile in the Cumyns'. Grants versus Comyns was one of our favourite games. I wonder if any Grant children play it now?

In 1424, although William Mackintosh of Mackintosh had apparently regained occupation of Connage in the Laich of Moray, a member of the Comyn family was still Keeper of Inverness Castle and still occupied Geddes and Rait. According to Sir Aeneas and the Macfarlane genealogies, Comyn, acting as Keeper of Inverness Castle, hanged several of Mackintosh's men 'for very slight cause'. Malcolm Mackintosh, who had lately (in 1411) fought at Bloody Harlaw on the side of the Lord of the Isles, entered the Castle of Nairn, where some of the principal Comyns were feasting, and killed them all. In Macfarlane's account, Mackintosh himself took the leading part in this exploit. In reprisal, the Comyns who, according to Sir Aeneas, numbered 1800 men, 'in a hostile manner' assaulted Mackintosh's lands in Strathdearn. Mackintosh, with 400 men, was on the island in Loch Moy and the Comyns built a dam across the outlet from the loch into the Funtack burn. Finding that he and his men were running out of provisions, Mackintosh 'landed silently' and there was a fight.[7]

According to the popular version, as told in the *New Statistical Account*, the Mackintoshes had been driven for refuge onto the island and were in danger of being drowned as the Comyn's dam caused the waters of the loch to rise. An ingenious clansman, having supplied himself 'with corks or wooden plugs and twine', at dead of night floated himself on a raft to this dam, bored holes in the boards of which it was made, inserted plugs to which he had fastened lengths of twine and gave them all at once such a tug that the plugs were pulled out. In the rush of water, the boards of the dam were carried away and the whole Comyn army which, most conveniently, had been encamped just below the dam, was engulfed. The ingenious clansman also perished. In confirmation of this yarn, the late Mackintosh of Mackintosh told me that a man, who claimed to be a descendant of the clansman who destroyed the dam, was still living on his estate at Dalcross. It has also been claimed that vestiges of an ancient wooden dam were found at the mouth of the burn. One wonders why, having had the means to retreat to this island, the Mackintoshes did not escape from it to make a stand instead of being nearly drowned like rats in a pail. Moreover, the Comyns must have been incredibly inefficient in posting guards to have allowed the dam above their camp to be destroyed. One also wonders if the dam had not been made by the Mackintoshes themselves in order to deepen the loch and make the island more inaccessible.

The clan comes better out of this episode in Macfarlane's account. Malcolm Mackintosh of Mackintosh, after his exploit in the Castle of Nairn, prepared for trouble. He chose 200 of his best men and, with them 'lurking in the wood' beside Loch Moy, waited for the Comyns. When they were seen to be coming to attack him, he ordered 'some of his men with the cattle, to flee to the hills in sight of the enemy that they might have no occasion to suspect a snare'. Some of the Comyns went in pursuit, the rest, their attention diverted, were completely off their guard and Malcolm, choosing his moment, dashed out with the rest of his men and attacked. Taken by surprise, the Comyns broke and fled. Numbers were killed in the rout and heaps of stones, that were placed over their bodies, 'bear witness to this day'.[8] Sir Aeneas gives a rather different account of this fight. Another myth disposes of the Comyns in a different way. Their leader treacherously invited the Chief of the Mackintoshes and his leading men to a feast at the Castle of Rait, planning to assassinate them at a given signal. Each Mackintosh guest was to be placed next to a Comyn and, when a bull's head, as part of the feast, was carried in they were to be killed. Everyone was made to swear to tell no one of the plot but a girl among the Comyns, who was in love with a young Mackintosh, trysted him at 'the Grey Stone of Croy' and then, while he listened, told the *Stone* of the plan. When the bull's head was carried in the Mackintoshes were quicker than the Comyns and each one dirked his neighbour. According to one version it was a Comyn man who warned his girl-friend. The tale of a treacherous massacre at the signal of the carrying of a bull's head is not unique to the Comyn-Mackintosh feud.

It was not, however, till 1442 that Malcolm was able to obtain a charter for Geddes and Rait. So ended the feud with the Comyns. The earlier family group, by the end of the period, had developed into a clan as we understand the word to mean, i.e. a definite type of social organization.

Moy and Clan Affairs

The defeat of the Comyns in 1424 was followed by the reappointment of Mackintosh of Mackintosh as Keeper of Inverness Castle (in 1428) and the reoccupation of Geddes, Rait and Petty by 1442. Connage had been regained before the final struggle. The Mackintoshes therefore, by the middle of the fifteenth century, had completely regained all that they had lost to the Comyns. One must now regard them as a clan and not a family and their complicated and turbulent history involved them in affairs far outwith Strathdearn. The chiefs styled themselves 'of Connage' (in the Laich of Moray) and then later 'of Dunachton' (in Badenoch) or less often 'of Torcastle' (in Strath Nairn), denoting their chief place of residence. Moy they visited in the summer for hunting and because Strathdearn contained valuable summer pasturage. It was not till the beginning of the eighteenth century that it became their permanent place of residence.

An account follows of the few tales about what actually happened in Strathdearn during these two hundred and fifty years, and then a brief general history of the clan so that anyone who wishes can easily skip it.

The first of these local incidents happened in 1454. It was an isolated quarrel with the Munroes, a clan with which the Mackintoshes had no long-standing feud. According to Highland custom any group of raiders going through the lands of another chief paid him a 'raiders collop'. Malcolm (10th), the leader in the battle against the Comyns, was living in his old age on the island in Loch Moy when a party of Munroes, led by the tutor of Foulis, came through Strathdearn on their way home from a raid into Perthshire.

Malcolm's grandson, another Malcolm (the son of his fourth son) was staying with him and, apparently acting very much on his own initiative, this very junior member of the family went to demand the 'raiders collop'. He was offered twenty-four cows and a bull. The young men who were with him incited him to refuse this and the Munroes continued on their way. Young Malcolm thereupon called out all the men he could in Strathdearn and Petty and set off in pursuit. In those days the Burgh of Inverness did not extend across the River Ness and the Munroes must have crossed the river and made their way along the further bank because young Malcolm and his men came up with them when they had just reached the Beauly Firth, where the village of Clachnaharry now stands. There was a fight, with many casualties, and young Malcolm himself lost the use of an arm. According to their own history, the Munroes took their revenge – they captured the Island of Moy and killed everyone on it – but the loyal historian of clan Mackintosh, A.M. Mackintosh, dismisses this story.[9] In spite of his daring exploit nothing more seems to be known of young Malcolm except that he married a Munro. A good many people have wondered what the obelisk set up on the rocky bluff above Clachnaharry commemorates. It was erected in 1821 by Major Duff of Muirtown to commemorate this rather unimportant fight. This is the story, as told me, but there are different versions of the details.

Another incident connected with Strathdearn took place in 1524. Sir Aeneas in his memoirs gives a good account of it. An over-indulgent Chief, Lachlan (14th), had given Connage, part of his most valuable property to an illegitimate nephew, named John, that thereby he might get Effy, the widow of Andrew Munro of Milton, in marriage. John, however, 'being a man much given to acts of robbery and opression', was told by his uncle that, if he did not alter his conduct, he would take Connage from him. Whereupon John resolved to murder his innocent uncle and Chief, which he 'did without delay, when he was at his hunting seat at the heights of Ruthven' (i.e. in the rough country at the end of the road that leads off the main road at Dalmagarry) alone, and without suspicion of harm, on the 25 March 1524. But, within a short time, by the alertness of Donald Glas Mackintosh, brother's son to the murdered Chief, i.e. his nephew, and two others, the murderer was caught and imprisoned on Loch an Eilean. Eventually, in the presence of the Earl of Moray, Lieutenant of the North, he was 'beheaded and dismembered on the south side of the Loch of Rothemurchus, also his associates were apprehended and being tortured were deservedly put to death and their heads and hands set upon poles where they had murdered their Chief'.[10]

A further story which did not actually happen at Moy took place not very far off, though Strathdearn people who took part in it must have come this way. When Mary Queen of Scots, in one of the brief spells of happiness that she had in Scotland, rode so gaily at the head of her troops to overawe Huntly and make her presence felt in the North, she found, when she reached Inverness, that the royal castle was, by Huntly's orders, being held against her and that his son, Sir John Gordon (to whom, according to rumour, Huntly wished to marry the Queen) was in command of insurgent forces only about ten miles off, near the present village of Ardersier. The loyal notables of the north hastened to come to her support, none more eagerly than young Lachlan Mor Mackintosh. He was still a minor and his education had been completed by a stay at court. He was the first to arrive and he guarded the Queen that night and meanwhile, by his orders, his tutor sent an urgent summons to all the men of Clan Chattan in Strathdearn, Strath Nairn and Petty to come to the Queen's defence. 'They came to the town in good order and undertook the Queen's protection'. By morning, Lovat and other chiefs with their men were arriving. The castle was captured and its Keeper hanged but, meanwhile young Lachlan had hurried off to intercept his clansmen in Strath Spey whom, Huntly's factor was calling out as his vassels to join his son's forces. Lachlan reached them as they were crossing the Nairn – they must have come by the Slochd and through the gap in the hills where the Parliamentary road crosses Strath Nairn between Meallmore and Daviot. The loyalty of clanship prevailed over all others and he brought them all back with him to serve the Queen. Huntly had murdered Lachlan's father and it must have been one of the sweetest hours in Lachlan Mor's life.

Fortunately, one can go along the road happily savouring the memory of outstanding events without following the complicated actions and reactions of two chains of events in the history of Clan Mackintosh affecting the clan as a whole. Two long sequences of trouble resulted from the marriage of Angus and Eva and had already begun to manifest themselves. One was the claim to the Chiefship of Clan Chattan. It may be noted that, besides the original Lochaber members of this confederation who had all moved with Mackintosh into his lands in Badenoch, other clans had joined. Two early and staunch supporters who were closely associated with Strathdearn, are the Macbeans and Macgillivrays. Another member of the confederation, also closely associated with the Strath, who joined rather later, is the MacQueen family. Very serious trouble was developing because the Macphersons, who had moved from Lochaber to Badenoch and had prospered there, claimed that their chief was also the Chief of Clan Chattan. They did so because Mackintosh based his claim upon descent from Eva, the heiress, that is descent in the female line, whereas Macpherson claimed descent in the male line from Gillichattan Mor.

The dispute for the Chiefship of Clan Chattan went on all through our period with great bitterness. There were meetings and discussions and, on one occasion, at least, a threat of civil war. In 1672 the Lord Lyon gave a formal ruling in favour of Mackintosh but the dispute was continued. The rights and wrongs of the dispute must have been hotly discussed by the families in Strathdearn, Kyllachie, Corriebrough and the rest, for their signatures consistently appear in deeds and agreements on the subject.[11]

The second legacy from Eva and Angus's stay in Lochaber had already started a feud with the Camerons and an apparent obsession by the Chiefs of Mackintosh to regain his lands there. It had already been shown by William (7th), an apparently astute and able man. This feud was carried on and led to further complications. As already noted Lochaber had been granted by Robert the Bruce to Angus Og of Islay, whose son assumed the title and semi-independent status of Lord of the Isles. Mackintosh became his vassal for the lands he held there. The Lord of the Isles confirmed his right and also granted him further land, that of Glen Roy, with certain rights of heritable jurisdiction. These claims to lands that had come to be occupied by the Macdonalds of Keppoch, led to another long and bitter feud which, like that with the Camerons, outlasted the existence of the Lordship of the Isles itself which was finally forfeited at the end of the fifteenth century.

The relationship between Mackintosh and the Lord of the Isles is an interesting one. Malcolm, the Chief who routed the Comyns at Moy, had already fought for Donald, the second Lord of the Isles, at Red Harlaw but, until the forfeiture of the Lordship at the very end of the fifteenth century, Mackintosh's attitude towards it was ambivalent. Sometimes he obtained an empty confirmation of rights that could never be permanently enforced; at other times he supported the royal forces. All this does not directly concern the people of Strathdearn. It is, however, of general interest that outwith the Lordship itself there was a line of clans impervious to its influence, the Mackenzies, the Frasers and Campbells: like them the Mackintoshes remained unaffected by its social and cultural influence.

During nearly the whole of our period the feud with the Camerons and Macdonald of Keppoch flared up again and again. There were about half-a-dozen large-scale raids and acts of retaliation. The Badenoch lands were more accessible for such counter-raids, but I wonder if the two large ovens that Sir Aeneas says were *discovered* (they had evidently long gone out of use) in 1780 on the island in Loch Moy, had not been used to bake bread (I suppose oatmeal bread, for wheat flour was a luxury) for some of their early expeditions. Of course, when the manpower of Clan Chattan was called out, the men of Strathdearn took their part.

In telling stories about feuds it is important to have some idea of the strength of the clan. It increased very greatly during our period. In the final fight with the Comyns, Mackintosh is said to have had 400 men. In fighting in the seventeenth century a chief was able to call up 1500 men. At the funeral of the nineteenth Chief in 1704, 2000 clansmen carrying arms attended.

This increase in manpower was not due to a proportional increase in the land that Mackintosh held. In Strathdearn itself, as we have seen, a great deal of the land was feued by members of the clan directly from the Earl of Moray. In Strath Nairn, the Macgillivrays, who were to play such an important role in the '45, held their land from Campbell of Cawdor. In many other cases in the same way, clansmen did not hold their land from the Chief. The extent to which the strong and warlike Clan Mackintosh held together, largely independently of a territorial tie, is almost unique in the history of Highland clans. Bishop Lesley, writing in the sixteenth century, said that the custom of Clan Chattan, as of many others, in the Irish Country (the Highlands) has been at all times to acknowledge one principle for their chief captain, to whom they are obedient in times of war and peace, for he is mediator between them and the prince. He defends them against the invasion of their enemies, their neighbours' and he causes minister justice to them all in manner of the country so that none should be suffered to make spoil or go sorning as they call it, or as vagabonds in the country.[12]

One can only speculate as to Mackintosh's income. He farmed some land and presumably got rent from relations planted on it. But most of his clansmen had to pay rent or feu duties to other people. Sir Aeneas says that he had the traditional due of the best animal of a deceased clansman and probably, like other chiefs, he received contributions towards extra expenses. On the other hand, it seems to have been customary for a chief to provide for the dependents of those killed in his service and liberal hospitality was certainly expected.

This is especially remarkable because Mackintosh's own position as a landowner was a weak one because he held so little land directly from the Crown – only the Barony of Moy, Church land granted to him after the Reformation and the lands in Lochaber from which he was never able to reap any benefit. The tenures by which he held his lands in the Laich of Moray, Petty, Connage, Geddes, Rait, the most valuable lands that he had, were so weak that by the eighteenth century he had lost them although some loyal members of the clan continued to live there. For short periods the chiefs had acquired other scattered portions of land, such as Culloden and holdings in the Aird, but at later dates they were obliged to sell them.

The connection with the upper valley of the Spey was an old one and it became more important. As we have seen, in very early days the family had been granted a lease of Rothiemurchus from the Bishop of Moray, but it had been virtually given to Shaw, the leader in the Battle of the Inches at Perth. Then, when King Robert the Bruce distributed the spoils of war after Bannockburn, Randolf, who had been made Earl of Moray, granted Mackintosh the lands of Benchar in Badenoch. It is not clear exactly by what tenure he made the grant or how far Benchar then extended. It must have been very considerable because all the members of Clan Chattan left Lochaber and came to settle in Badenoch, in addition to several Mackintosh cadets who became established in Badenoch and Rothiemurchus.

Unfortunately, a serious complication arose because of the weakness of his position in holding his lands. Mackintosh had held his lands in the Laich of Moray as a vassal of the Earl of Moray. There had been disagreements – I referred to one earlier – but, on the whole, the relationship had been good. But in 1451 the King reappointed a feudal superior over Badenoch and the Earl of Huntly received the Lordship and became Mackintosh's superior for his lands there. As a sort of addendum one may point out that this unsatisfactory position had one advantage. One of Privy Council orders most resented by Highland land-lords was the constantly renewed one that made them responsible for their vassals; Mackintosh at least once, in 1635, was able to escape responsibility by pleading that he held all his land of superiors.

The Gordon family was very much on the upgrade. Gordon was only created Earl of Huntly in 1449. In 1509 he had received lands in Lochaber and he had thus been able to make a great deal of trouble in Mackintosh's efforts to gain possession of his own lands there. During the sixteenth century, the Earldom of Moray changed hands and underwent a series of misfortunes; for a short time Huntly was actually Earl of Moray (1548-54). The Lordship of the Isles having been forfeited there was no other real grandee so that Huntly became, in his own terms, 'Cock of the North'. Relations between Mackintosh and Huntly were on the whole good until the middle of the sixteenth century. By then, Mackintosh had acquired what he obviously regarded as his most desirable possession, for he began to take his style from it and to be known as Mackintosh of Dunachton.

Feu holding is still an ordinary form of tenure of land in Scotland. One pays one's feu duty in the same way as one pays one's rent. It meant something very different in the Highlands in the sixteenth century. One story, which illustrates the kind of society that formed the background to the constant succession of warlike episodes in the history of Clan Mackintosh, will suffice. It is told in Macfarlane's *Genealogical Collections*.[13] It is a good, almost contemporary, example of current ideas of feudal obligations. Huntly and the Earl Marischal had had a quarrel. The Earl Marischal had boasted that he was as good as Huntly in wealth and power. Huntly had retorted that he had a vassal who would exterminate him from the bounds of the Mearns (a district in Kincardineshire where the Earl had much property). As soon as Huntly got home he told Mackintosh what had happened and ordered him 'by spoliation or in some other humiliating way to disgrace Marischal'. Mackintosh forthwith took the matter in hand and sent his son with 600 strong men to the Mearns. Without a fight they 'brought the booty', i.e. drove the cattle 'of the whole of the Mearns to the gates of Strathbogie Castle'. Huntly was much pleased, but soon afterwards he went too far in his demands of Mackintosh. He wished to enforce the payments of his revenues in Badenoch (some of them from Mackintosh) and he therefore planned to repair Ruthven Castle, on the hillock just opposite Kingussie (where the ruins of the eighteenth-century barracks now stand). He required of Mackintosh that his tenants and friends would assist the architect and Huntly's servants in the work by 'carrying stones, timber, lime and other necessaries'. Mackintosh replied that he was 'nowise bound' to render such services and 'utterly refused'.

It is against such a background that I make the excuse for re-telling the most dramatic tale about the Mackintoshes because the Barony of Moy and Schephin were among the lands forfeited and then restored to the Chief. Relations with Huntly deteriorated, especially after Mackintosh was able to acquire the valuable lands of Dunachton by marrying one of the joint heiresses to this old Macniven property. Huntly became jealous. There are two versions of what followed.

According to the story told by Sir Walter Scott in *Tales of a Grandfather*, the Chief of Clan Mackintosh had incurred the wrath of the Earl of Huntly because of certain acts of lawless aggression and the powerful Earl was preparing to call out his forces to exact vengeance on the wrongdoers. In order to save his clan, the Chief of Mackintosh decided to surrender himself to Huntly's vengeance but, thinking that Lady Huntly would be more merciful than her lord, he went to his castle (Strathbogie) when he knew that Huntly would be absent. The lady was supervising the cutting up of the winter's supply of meat in preparation for salting it (owing to the inadequacy of winter feeding this was a regular Scots custom). She received Mackintosh's plea for forgiveness coldly and told him that her lord had sworn never to forgive him till his neck was laid on the block. Mackintosh replied that he would stoop even to that and give his life to save his clan and, kneeling down, he laid his head on the block on which the joints of meat were being cut up. The lady, unmoved, made a sign to the cook who immediately cut off his head with his cleaver. In punishment for this murder, according to the printed story, Huntly had to give up to Mackintosh Dunachton, Lynwilg and Schephin and, in the tale as told locally, Lynwilg was known as 'the Davoch of the Head'. I was told, however, that Huntly did not give up Dunachton to Mackintosh (for it belonged to the Macnivens) but gave him the right to marry the Macniven heiress. As a matter of fact, a former Chief, the uncle of the one murdered by Huntly, had secured from Huntly the gift of the marriage of the Macniven heiress for his son who had to obtain the assent of Huntly by giving him a bond of man-rent. It is interesting that this factual detail should have survived in the folktale.

The true story is that when Huntly began to show enmity to Mackintosh, a degenerate cousin (whose father was the murderer of an earlier Chief in one of the two tales already told about Moy) went to Huntly and accused Mackintosh (William, 15th) of conspiring to murder him. Huntly took up the charge. He managed to seize Mackintosh in 1550 and brought him to Aberdeen for trial on the charge of practising against the life of the Queen's Lieutenant in the North (himself). He, himself, was also the judge, and the jury was a picked one of his supporters and the witnesses were all Mackintosh's proven enemies. Mackintosh protested at the composition of the jury and at the people who had been summoned to give evidence. The Provost of Aberdeen,

Thomas Menzies, made a courageous protest against the trial and, his protest being unheeded, he publicly appealed to Parliament and left the court. Huntly ignored him, proceeded with the trial and pronounced sentence that Mackintosh was guilty and that therefore all his possessions were forfeited and that his head should be struck from his body. The Provost immediately convened the town in arms to prevent the execution and Huntly carried Mackintosh off as his prisoner to Strathbogie. He then left for France where he had been ordered to attend the Queen Dowager but, in the words of the Kinrara MS, he left Mackintosh to his lady to deal with and she had him beheaded in 1550.

On his return, Huntly arranged that the forfeited lands, including Moy and Schephin, should be granted to his own son. He also rewarded the kinsman who had betrayed Mackintosh who, however, did not live to benefit by the grant for members of the clan killed him. At that moment it was the only thing that they could do to avenge their Chief. The efforts of Mackintosh's friends and relations – and by marriage he had kinsfolk in very high places, including the Earl of Cassillis – failed to bring Huntly to justice. Eventually, in 1554, fate helped them. Huntly, who was high in the Queen's favour, was ordered to proceed against Clan Ranald. His Lowland vassals refused to venture into the Highlands while he, himself, was afraid to call out his Highland ones so he had to give up the expedition. The Queen was furious and ordered that he should be imprisoned while an enquiry was held. At this point, Cassillis and Mackintosh's other friends had the backing of the Protestant party because Huntly was a Roman Catholic. He was accused of being the prime cause of all the trouble in the North, besides the beheading of the Laird of Mackintosh, and he was banished for a short period, fined and deprived of the Earldom of Moray which had lately been granted to him. It was not, however, until 1557 that Cassillis was able to summon Huntly and his son to appear before Parliament to hear his verdict, pronounced against Mackintosh at Aberdeen, 'reduced, rescinded and annulled'. The sentence of death was declared to be illegal and the restitution of the forfeited lands was made by charters for them all including, of course, Moy and Schephin.

One has to remember that Lachlan Mor (16th), the Chief who came to the rescue of Mary Queen of Scots, as I have told, was the son of the murdered Chief in order to appreciate the triumph the young man must have felt when he brought Huntly's Badenoch vassals to serve the Queen. In 1675 Lachlan (19th) built a new house at Dunachton. It was the family headquarters and, but for one incident in the long drawn-out feud with the Lochaber clans, one wonders if Moy would ever have become the permanent home of the Chiefs of Clan Mackintosh instead of their summer residence.

As well as trouble with Huntly, the Chiefs of Mackintosh, when they felt able, periodically tried to make good their claims to rule and jurisdiction in parts of Lochaber, but the feud with the Camerons ended dramatically in 1665. Men from Strathdearn certainly took part in this final episode. Mackintosh (Lachlan, 19th) was described in the unfriendly pages of Sir Aeneas Macpherson's *Loyall Dissuasive* as 'arrogant'. He certainly was exceedingly active. A number of meetings and conferences were held, one of which is amusingly described by Master James Fraser in the *Wardlaw Manuscript*. It took place close to Inverness. Mackintosh was supported by the Earl of Moray, the Provost of Inverness, his uncle and other gentlemen of the clan. Cameron of Lochiel had, as his supporters, Lord Lovat and a number of Frasers. Mackintosh, with 500 of his men, was encamped on the east side of the river; Lochiel, with 300 men, on the west side near Tomnahurich. 'Earth, water, aire, rebounded at the sound of bagpipes martial musick. At the sound of a trumpet the meeting sits.' But the Bishop of Moray and the Laird of Altyre had to act as 'Trenchmen' and pass between the two groups of contestants. On the third day matters were brought to 'an accommodation and agreement'. Master James adds: 'This was a noble sight of gallant gentlemen and the clergy in decent grave garbs.'[14]

It was, however only one of many abortive attempts to reach an understanding. Finally Lachlan (19th) felt justified in using force. He called out Clan Chattan, marched into Lochaber with a force made up of members of Clan Chattan and other allies, totalling 1500 men, and camped on the north side of Loch Arkaig. Cameron of Lochiel, with 1200 men, was prepared to defend his lands but first he made an offer of 72,000 merks to Mackintosh. This offer Kyllachie and Corriebrough (Corriebrough Mor, now Balnespick) urged Mackintosh to accept, but he refused it as 'a naughty inconsiderate rate'. As the opening of hostilities became imminent an emissary from Argyll appeared upon the scene, a young John Campbell, later on the very astute Lord Breadalbane. He had financial backing from Argyll and commanded 300 men. He was kin to both Chiefs and he told them that, if either of them refused to make peace, he would join forces with the other and attack him. Mackintosh, again urged by Kyllachie and Corriebrough Mor, most unwillingly accepted the offer that Lochiel had already made (72,000 merks equalled about £48,300 Scots − £4,025 Sterling). Argyll guaranteed that the money would be paid and he did so himself in 1666. Mackintosh gave up his claims and Lochiel continued to occupy the lands, holding them from Argyll instead of Mackintosh. The incident is of some general interest because it is one of the few recorded examples of politics within a clan. The recollection that Mackintosh had been over-ruled evidently rankled. Sir Aeneas, generally so tactful, writing more than a century later says that Lachlan sold the lands and 'by this ill-advice of some of his relations'. He notes that the sum paid was 70,000 merks.

During the lifetime of the same Chief (Lachlan 19th) the feud with the Macdonalds for lands in Lochaber was also brought to an end. The events leading up to this very much affected Moy and its future. The grants to Mackintosh of certain lands in Lochaber, Glen Roy and Glen Spean, and of hereditary jurisdiction over them, had been made by the Lord of the Isles and confirmed by the Crown, but at the same time they had actually become the patrimony of the Macdonalds of Keppoch. Lachlan Mackintosh (19th), in pursuance of the claim, had obtained in 1681 from the Scots Privy Council a Commission of Fire and Sword against Keppoch, but he obviously had not felt that he had sufficient backing to enforce it so he continued to negotiate with Keppoch. While the negotiations were going on Keppoch died and was succeeded by his son, Coll, who was still a student at St Andrews University. There are two sides to a good deal of what followed. Coll, apparently in good faith, went to Inverness to discuss the claims and Lachlan Mackintosh, with somewhat dubious right, apparently based on his rights of jurisdiction in Lochaber, had him arrested and lodged in Inverness Tolbooth. The loyal historian of Clan Mackintosh suggests that Inverness Town Council were behind the action for there was bitter animosity between the townsmen and many branches of the Macdonalds. Coll appealed to the Scots Privy Council who ordered that he be instantly released. A letter from Huntly shows that action by the Privy Council was taken because of pressure from him and that he was turning the incident to account to weaken the Mackintosh's position in Lochaber where he himself was trying to gain more influence. Coll was released but thenceforward he bore a bitter grudge against both Lachlan Mackintosh and the burgh of Inverness. Lachlan, continuing his attempts to gain recognition for his claims, at last induced the Privy Council to order the citizens of Inverness to support him and also to send a contingent of troops. With those auxiliaries and the manpower of Clan Chattan – with the exception of the Macphersons – Lachlan marched into Lochaber. Among his clansmen that we know were there were the sons of Kyllachie and Aberarder and no doubt many more men from Strathdearn. Coll outmanoeuvred him and secured a position ideal for a downhill charge, the most effective form of Highland attack at this point in history. A townsman of Inverness, a tobacco spinner who had joined the expedition, has left an account of the battle. He described how Keppoch's men came down the hill without shoes or stockings or bonnets. They gave a shout and attacked with swords and Lochaber axes. When he saw men with cleft heads all around him and, being fiercely attacked himself, he beat off his assailant, took to his heels and ran thirty miles without looking back. Lachlan and his force were utterly defeated and, according to one account, he himself was taken prisoner. As a prime humiliation he was rescued by the Macphersons although they had refused to follow him. The battle of Mulroy, fought in 1688, was still remembered in Glen Roy when I was a girl. I often used to stay there and my hostess, herself a Macdonald of Keppoch, used glee-fully to point out the heathery slope and the green patches on it that marked the graves of the slain Mackintoshes. Mulroy is said to have been the last pitched clan battle and also the earliest recorded example of the downhill charge. In punishment for his action against a force that included levies raised on the order of the Privy Council, that body took more vigorous action against Coll and regular troops were sent to Lochaber and harried his lands.

Coll, however, was soon able to seize an opportunity of settling his old scores with Lachlan Mackintosh and Inverness. He joined Dundee in the Rising in support of James VII against William of Orange, but he did so on his own terms. He appeared in force before the town of Inverness, seized some of its leading citizens and held them as hostages, threatening to sack the town unless a large sum of money was paid to him. Dundee had to rush north. He gave a promissory note for the money Coll had already secured (but it had to be paid later by the Scots Parliament). He also tried to heal the quarrel between Coll and Lachlan for he was anxious to gain the armed support of Clan Mackintosh. Lachlan, however, refused to meet Coll and took no part in the Rising.

James Philip, in his roseate account of Dundee's Highland following in his *Grameid*, describes Coll as 'accustomed to pillage and unjust rapine' and his men as 'of fierce aspect' and to whom 'life in arms alone is pleasing and to drive the new booty a delight'.[15]

Before joining Dundee's army, Keppoch took the opportunity of raiding the lands of members of Clan Chattan in Strath Nairn — Macgillivray, Macbean and others — and, obviously using the gap long afterwards followed by the Parliamentary part of our road, he broke into Strathdearn and pillaged Mackintosh's lands round Moy. He also used the pass further up to harry the lands of Dalmigavie who had lost two sons at Mulroy. Driving his plunder before him, he could easily cross from the head of Strath Nairn through Strath Errick to the Great Glen and so to Lochaber.

Later in Dundee's campaign, Coll had a second chance of revenging himself upon Lachlan. As Dundee was marching with his army down Badenoch he looked back and saw clouds of smoke behind him. Coll had turned back, burned down the new house at Dunachton that Lachlan had only recently built and was harrying his lands. Dundee was furious and had Coll up before his assembled officers and told him that he would much rather choose to serve as a common soldier with disciplined troops than command men who disgraced the cause that they served by their conduct. Coll apologized and fought for Dundee at Killiecrankie.[16] In his petition to the Scots Parliament against Coll Macdonald of Keppoch, Lachlan Mackintosh gave a vivid picture of the desolation Coll wrought in the two raids. Beside destroying Dunachton and the outbuildings, Keppoch "did harrie and robb his haille Lands in Badzenoch, Strathnairn and Stratherne, thereby exposing the pet^r to a vast loss and his tennents to beggarie, whereby his haill lands are laid waste and will so continue until the pet^r be in a condition to replenish them'. In a further petition there was a list of the lands which included Moy and Schephin. The tenants and possessors were said to have had to flee for their lives and, with their wives and children, were begging their bread and living upon charity. Mackintosh was exempted from paying cess while the lands remained waste.

These raids had important consequences for the future of Moy because the destruction of Dunachton, which he had obviously regarded as his permanent home, so unsettled Mackintosh that he and his son made other arrangements. For the time being, no effective action was taken against Coll Macdonald of Keppoch until, at last, in 1697 King William himself took the matter up and wrote to the Scots Privy Council telling them that they must enforce the law and restore the lands to Mackintosh as their rightful owner. Letters of Fire and Sword were issued against the Macdonalds of Keppoch, the fencible men from the five adjoining counties were called up, and a garrison of regular troops was established in the newly established post of Fort William.

Coll Macdonald now came to terms and, in 1700, signed a submission on behalf of himself and his people to Mackintosh. He himself left the country for a time and the people paid their rents more or less regularly to Mackintosh. And so ended the feud.[17]

Lachlan Mackintosh had built a house on the island in Loch Moy in 1665. It was, of course, the period of the great cattle-droving trade and, as we have seen, about half-a-dozen leading men of the clan settled permanently in Strathdearn about that time. It is evident from Sir Aeneas's description of the house as having 'four fire rooms', i.e. rooms with fireplaces, and from the ruins of its foundations, that it was not one of the traditional Scots 'tower houses', with a ground story designed for defence, a great hall and the adornment of these turrets that Bryce and his followers copied so zealously in their Victorian Scottish baronial style. On the contrary, I like to think of it as an early example of a house built for the greater privacy and amenity in living that was becoming usual; it is in agreeable contrast to the stormy life that Lachlan (19th) had had to live.

After the destruction of Dunachton, he obtained a wadset of Dalcross Castle (near the present airfield) in 1688 for his winter quarters and his son bought this castle outright later on. Lachlan became dissatisfied with the house on the island in Loch Moy and, about 1700, he built a new house on the shores of the loch. Sir Aeneas made a drawing of it. It is a plain, well-proportioned Georgian type of house that was to be the scene of so many happenings affecting the lives of the people along the road. Lachlan died at Dalcross, old and worn-out. He had been Chief a long time – forty-four years – many of them the most decisive in the history of the clan.

This seems to be the best place to make a brief reference to a fanciful tale about 'The Curse of Moy'. A.M. Mackintosh[18] gives a sketch of two versions, both of which purport to be founded upon tradition, but neither of which can be collated to any names of people who actually existed. For instance, the second version is told in connection with events that happened in 1378, whereas the victims, the family of Grants of Glen Urquhart and Glen Moriston, were not in existence until about a hundred and fifty years after that. One version of the tale is given in a poem by Morritt of Rokeby written in 1802. According to it, the Mackintosh Chief of the day had become enamoured with Margaret,

Moy Hall the Seat of the Chief of the Mackintoshes 550 miles, ...

Old Moy Hall sketched by Sir Aeneas Mackintosh about 1775.

daughter of Grant of Glen Urquhart and Glen Moriston, and had been rejected by her. He had somehow captured her, her father and her accepted suitor, Grant of Alva, and had imprisoned them in his castle on Loch Moy. Margaret, by tears and entreaties, persuaded him to release one of the two men (while killing the other) and leaving the choice of who should perish to her. Her father urged her to save the life of her lover and to let him himself die. Mackintosh had expected that her father would persuade her to save his own life at the expense of that of her lover. He was furious, had both men killed and their bodies shown to the girl. She went mad – for years she haunted the cairns erected over the bodies of the two men in some place in the hills. (This is mixed up with a Badenoch tradition about a woman buried in the cleft in the Cairngorms where the snow is the last to melt; it is known as the *Ciste Mhairearaid*, the Coffin of Margaret). She also called down a curse on Mackintosh:

> Never the son of a Chief of Moy
> Might live to protect his father's age
> Or close in peace his dying eye
> Or gather his gloomy heritage

A.M. Mackintosh does not give the reference for the other version. According to it, Margaret only cursed Mackintosh and not his descendants. He was to 'die a bloody death leaving neither wife nor child', leaping from his castle ramparts and drowning in the loch. The story then states that, about 1378, in reprisal for a fight in which the wicked Mackintosh Chief had killed a Munro, a number of Munroes forced their way into the castle at Moy and killed everyone within it. This is pure fiction. In the eighteenth century, the road past Loch Moy was to echo with alarms and excursions from actual and far greater conflicts.

The '15

Early in the eighteenth century Moy was becoming the main residence of Mackintosh of Mackintosh and his family. A strange mixture of events connected with the past, the present and the future took place in and around the unpretentious-looking house, as Moy then was, on the peaceful loch shore. As a legacy from quarrels of the past, in 1724 a meeting was held at Moy to clinch the vexed question of the Chiefship of Clan Chattan.[19] In his own days there were the Jacobite claims to the throne that led to the Rising of 1715 and it was in discussions at Moy that the Chief was persuaded to call out his clan in an armed rising in support of the Jacobite cause. In a striking pre-vision of the future it was at Moy that, in his later years, the same Chief, Lachlan (20th), drew up a plan for a clan association that, although it was itself very short-lived, was an early example of future clan organisations.[20]

The Jacobite risings in '15 and '45 had profound effects upon the Highlands. They, of course, are part of the general history of Scotland and much of the action took place far from Strathdearn; but Strathdearn folk were personally deeply involved and in '46 part of the great tragedy was actually played out on the very ground one walked on.

The sympathies of Clan Mackintosh had been consistently loyalist during the Civil Wars. Although the Chief of the time was infirm, members of the clan (among them one of my mother's family) had been 'out' with Montrose. It was only because of the outrageous behaviour of Dundee's subordinate, Coll Macdonald of Keppoch, that the Chief did not bring out his clan in that Rising.

The very unlucky Rising of the '15 begun under the prime misfortune of having a leader as deficient in qualities of leadership as he was in principles. The Earl of Mar had made his name as an adroit politician in the negotiations that had preceded the Act of Union of 1707 and had earned the nickname of Bobbing Jock from the way in which he had constantly changed sides. After the death of Queen Anne he had tried to ingratiate himself with George I, her successor from Hanover, by collecting the signatures of many Highland Chiefs to a letter expressing loyalty to him. The new King, however, would have nothing to do with Mar and he therefore espoused the Jacobite cause and, as everyone knows, raised the Royal Standard, and proclaimed James VIII to be the rightful King, at Braemar on the 6th September 1715.

During the intrigues and negotiations that had preceded this, a man came upon the scene who was the very antithesis of Mar, above all in his complete integrity to the principles of loyalty – William Mackintosh the younger – of Borlum (the old Brigadier), some of whose adventures I have already retailed. He was not only kin to Mackintosh, there was a family friendship. Lachlan had graduated at St Andrews, but had been mainly occupied in looking after the estate as his father was in poor health. William was far older in the ways of the world. He had married a lady of Queen Anne's court. He had seen life soldiering on the continent. His considerable ability and energy were directed by the driving force of his fanatical loyalty to the House of Stuart. By the peaceful shores of the loch, and within the house there he 'prevailed on' Mackintosh (who is said to have 'delivered himself' up to him) to commit himself and his clan to armed rebellion against the established Government in the cause of 'the King over the water'. It is known that Mackintosh had a secret meeting with Glengarry, Chisholm of Comar and others 'within twelve miles of Inverness'. The obvious place is Moy.

Action followed within days of Mar's proclamation at Braemar. Mackintosh summoned a meeting of the men of Clan Chattan at Farr (in Strath Nairn) on the 14th September and from there marched on Inverness where James VIII was proclaimed King and supplies of public stores of arms, money and lead were collected. Young Borlum (the Brigadier) seems to have taken the main initiative. He is said to have made the actual proclamation and to have taken steps to hinder pro-Hanoverian clans from being summoned to join the Government forces. Then, without doing 'any further damage', Mackintosh and his forces left the town and marched to Culloden House to demand supplies of arms that were said to be stored there. Forbes of Culloden was away from home but his lady courageously refused to give them up. Without molesting her, Mackintosh set out to join the Jacobite army that was gathering at Perth. He had with him 800 well-armed men. They would naturally take the direct route over the hills, through the gap in the Monadh Liath where the Parliamentary part of our road runs, cross Strathdearn to the Slochd and march on to Drumochter. Kinsfolk and friends would greet them as they went, for Kyllachie himself and MacQueen of Corriebrough's son were certainly among them and they would bring a following of Strathdearn men. Eventually, a battalion was embodied of which Mackintosh himself was Colonel. In the list of thirty-two officers, twenty-eight had Clan Chattan names, Kyllachie and Corriebrough among them, and also two members of my mother's family from Badenoch.

Mackintosh's regiment formed part of a 'Highland Brigade' commanded by William Mackintosh, 'the Brigadier'. Weeks passed in muddles, indecision, divided councils and in inaction at Perth. Finally, the Highland Brigade was sent off to join Jacobite supporters raised in south-eastern Scotland and on to England, where for them the Rising ended. Mar, much later, with the rest of his forces, fought the indecisive battle of Sheriffmuir and returned to Perth where, in utter futility, the Rising withered away.

In the story of the Brigadier, I have outlined his preliminary expedition to Fife and across the Firth of Forth. He then, on instructions, joined the force partly made up of Jacobites from Dumfries and the West. Against all good advice, a Mr Forster (he is never given a military title) prevailed upon Mar to send this force into the north of England to try to win Jacobite support there. Very few men, however, joined and Forster allowed his small force to be penned in Preston by increasingly powerful bodies of regular troops. The Mackintosh regiment distinguished itself in holding one of the barricades that was hastily set up to resist an attack. The position was hopeless. Forster secretly planned an absolute surrender and the Highlanders, when they heard of it, rioted, preferring to die fighting. Mackintosh and Lord Derwentwater were sent as two hostages while the capitulation was arranged. In spite of protests, the final surrender was complete. The Jacobite force, numbering about 1500 men, was disarmed. The more important prisoners (including Mackintosh, the Brigadier, Kyllachie and young Corriebrough) were sent to London to stand trial for treason. We know a little about what happened to them. After the humiliating march through the London mob in which the Brigadier won respect, the prisoners were distributed among various jails. On the eve of the trial Kyllachie and young Corriebrough escaped from Newgate in women's clothes. After some delay we hear of them safely back in Strathdearn.

The Brigadier's escape was more sensational. Several other prisoners broke out of jail with him. Some were caught, three or four escaped. A member of my mother's branch of the clan was less fortunate. He was condemned to death but later reprieved. However, the expenses incurred in obtaining this ruined his family. Mackintosh himself was kept in prison till August. A.M. Mackintosh quotes a diary of a fellow inmate of Newgate Prison. 'The Laird of Mackintosh, the Chief of his Clan, was discharg'd upon the intercession of his Lady and others of his friends, who made it plain that he was trepann'd into the Rebellion by the craft of the Brigadier.' The prisoners in London were obviously well treated.

The lot of the lesser prisoners was harder. A.M. Mackintosh studied what little information he could find about them. They were distributed among prisons in the North of England and 'Many were shipped off to slavery in the American plantations.' Some of the officers, in order to obtain a pardon, were compelled to bind themselves for a term of service in America. The indenture of 'James Mackintosh of Kinrara, gentleman' survives. He had been a lieutenant in the Mackintosh regiment. He was the kinsman of my mother's ancestor. He bound himself for seven years to serve Henry Trafford, merchant of Liverpool, or his assigns in Virginia or other of His Majesty's plantations. He was assigned by Trafford to a plantation in Virginia. Among the rank and file who were sent to Liverpool for transportation or were executed or died in jail at Lancaster were sixty bearing Clan Chattan names, including thirteen Mackintoshes and sixteen Macgillivrays. We do not know if men from Strathdearn were among them. We do not know if any of them came back.

The activities of Lachlan were not limited to his participation in this disastrous expedition. The dispute with Cluny Macpherson over the Chiefship of Clan Chattan had reached, it was hoped, a final settlement. In 1724 a meeting had been held at Moy of the leading men of families belonging to Clan Chattan. They met, no doubt they feasted, a formal agreement was signed, but in a few years the claim to a dignity that was becoming of less and less practical importance was renewed by Cluny Macpherson.

Another enterprise by Lachlan, although a very short-lived one, is by far the earliest example that I have ever heard of, of a form of organization that, more than a hundred years later, was to become one of the most important forms of survival by the clan spirit. In 1727 Lachlan was planning to form a clan association. Its objects were stated to be:

1. to raise funds from which to pay the expenses of lawyers to deal with any legal action by or against Clan Chattan or any of its members. The need for this was stated to be because members of the clan 'liveing dispersed in severall cuntreys distant from one another and cannot act together';

2. to make provision for an arbitrator in clan disputes;

3. for meetings of the clan at which Mackintosh was to act as convener, to generally encourage unanimity, love and friendship among the clan and defend them in 'a lawful manner' from the insults and reproaches of others.

Members of the association were required to make a contribution to its funds. Mackintosh himself gave £2000. Others gave varying sums of lesser amounts down to twenty merks (£1.20). Among the contributors were Rob Smith and Ewan Macpherson 'wugmaker [wigmaker]', John Paul 'cutlier' and smaller contributions from Allec M'Intosh 'glover' and William M'Intosh 'hyrer'. It is not known how long the association lasted.

Lachlan (20th) died in 1731 at Moy but his body was taken to Dalcross

Castle where he had a magnificent funeral. He is said to have had a ready wit, was 'facetious' in his conversation and was an agreeable companion. He had no children and was succeeded by his second cousin, William.

The '45

The events of 1745-46 are happenings that are far beyond the scope of the associations strung along this bit of the road. Looking from the road to the loch-shore, one can only imagine what the house looked like in which Angus (22nd) Mackintosh of Mackintosh and his wife Anne (née Farquharson of Invercauld) lived. I do not think that written sources still exist that would clarify his real intentions and motives at a time of national crisis. Her portrait survives and one can assume that it gives a clue to her personality. The rather heavy features and generous mouth suggest that she was a strong-willed, good-hearted woman but, to me, the portrait does not convey the great personal charm that she obviously had. She was twenty when she married, young enough to act spontaneously in response to the immediacy of a crisis. She belonged to a strongly Jacobite family. According to her husband's nephew, who knew her well, as a girl she had pitied the Prince 'for his misfortunes which he had not brought on himself'.[21] Like most Scots of that time she probably shared in a general dislike of English interference in Scots affairs.

I think that the circumstances under which Angus had inherited his property help to explain his caution. When he succeeded his invalid brother the family finances were in an unsatisfactory condition. The last hundred years had been expensive and extravagant ones. All over the Highlands the chiefs and lesser gentry, trying to keep up with southern standards, had run into difficulty. We have seen how this had happened to the group of landowners higher up Strathdearn. With Mackintosh of Mackintosh there had been special expenses. Lachlan (19th) 1660-1704 had inherited feuds with the Camerons and the Macdonalds of Keppoch to prosecute which must have involved a great deal of expense. In compensation for land and rights given up to the Camerons he got a sum of money, but his lands were ravaged and his home burnt down by Keppoch and one doubts if the compensation he finally got from Parliament made up for the losses of stock and steadings to himself and his tenants. In spite of this loss, he bought a wadset of Dalcross Castle, a truly Scottish baronial, be-turreted abode and his family gave him a grandiose funeral. His body lay in state at Dalcross for over a month and cooks

Anne, Wife of Angus Mackintosh of Mackintosh (22nd Chief), 'Colonel Anne' of the '45. Portrait attributed to Allan Ramsay.

were brought from Edinburgh to supply the continuous funeral feasts. Beside 2000 armed men of his own clan, neighbouring chiefs brought contingents for the final ceremony and the funeral procession is said to have been four miles long.[22]

This Chief was succeeded by his son, another Lachlan (20th) 1704-31. He not only completed the purchase of Dalcross but he built a large new house on the loch shore at Moy. He was 'out' in the '15 and his imprisonment and the arrangements for his release must have cost a great deal. In 1724 he held a great gathering of Clan Chattan at Moy. He died in 1731 at Moy but the body was moved to Dalcross and lay there for two months until his heir and successor could arrive to make the funeral arrangements. There was lavish hospitality and 2000 armed men were present.

No wonder his successor William (21st) 1731-40, his second cousin, had to retrench. It was probably in his time that the reductions in the traditional attendants of a chief, that Sir Aeneas had noted, took place. They would most likely be accompanied by that of many lesser members of the staff. He had to go abroad for his health and he died in Edinburgh.

Angus (22nd), the Chief of Mackintosh at the time of the '45, was his brother. He had to sell a good deal of his most valuable land in Badenoch. The diminution in the status kept up by the Chief, which had been forced upon the two brothers, probably wounded the feelings of the clansmen. It is not easy for someone who is hard up to be a very generous landlord or play the part of the local grandee. One pictures him, from the scraps of information available, as canny and tenacious of what he was able to salvage of the family heritage. It may have been owing to a lack of leadership in dealing with other people and lack of personal popularity among his clansmen and tenantry, from whom he would have had to raise the quota of recruits, that may account for the fact that he was only a Captain in Sempill's Regiment in Loudon's army and did not raise a regiment himself (as his wife was to do!).[23] On the other hand the struggles he was making to repair the losses incurred by militant predecessors encouraged his natural caution and he may deliberately have taken an inconspicuous position safely on the Government side while tacitly allowing his wife to raise the clan to fight for the Prince.

There are several instances in the Jacobite Rising of members of a family — for instance brothers — taking opposite sides in order to safeguard the family estates. One has to remember that there was none of the religious and class bitterness that is so evident in the English Civil War.

But, so far as I know, it was unique for a husband and wife to be so active on opposite sides. Although 'Colonel Anne's' activities in raising a regiment were much noted, it is remarkable how little contemporary comment there is upon the piquant situation that her husband was actually serving upon the other side. One is left wondering if he was uxoriously weak or cold-bloodedly astute. It is fascinating that a copy of a letter from him survives that is completely out of character with either of these views of him. Ewan, son of Cluny Macpherson, had originally joined the Prince but, later on, transferred his allegiance to King George. While he was with the Jacobites it was reported that Prince Charles Edward offered him the command of the Clan Chattan Regiment, whereupon Mackintosh wrote him a furious letter saying that he was now thinking of joining the Prince's forces himself and had a mind to command his own people and risk the same fate as they, that he was willing to offer young Ewan the position of second-in-command and he warned him not to proceed with his projected command: 'do not put me to the necessity of requiring my men of you in a more publick maner, the consequence of which may be disagreeable to booth'.[24] It is a revelation of how completely things have changed in the Highlands that a threat to the position of Chief of Clan Chattan, now one of purely sentimental interest to a comparatively few people, should either have roused him from the utter domination of his wife or completely upset his extremely adroit manoeuvres.

The first taste of the coming struggle must have been when General Cope's army camped one night at Moy on his march to Inverness.[25] He was taking evasive action and going there instead of to Fort Augustus as he had originally intended in order to avoid a confrontation with Prince Charles Edward who had just landed on the mainland and was gathering a large following. Cope had met with great hostility from the local people as he passed through Perthshire. In Strathdearn, besides the more general anti-English feelings of the Scots, there was a tradition of Jacobite loyalty and local feelings were further embittered by the execution of three soldiers in the Black Watch, members of Clan Chattan – all Badenoch men – because of trouble in that regiment, largely due to official stupidity. One pictures the campfires of the soldiers beside the loch and up and down the Strath in the clusters of the farmsteads, unseen in the darkness, the rising blaze of fury that was to send the raising of 'Colonel Anne's' regiment off to a flying start.

Sir Aeneas, writing within living memory of the Rising, plays down the fables that had grown up about the military activities of Lady Mackintosh (as a landowner's wife was then called), fables that even represented her as riding a white horse at the head of her regiment on the battlefield. Even more absurd stories about her have grown up since his day. According to one, she upset a great pot of broth, that was hanging over the fire, over her husband's legs as he sat by the fire and so made him unable to raise and lead a regiment on the Hanoverian side. Needless to say people of any position in the Highlands by this period did not live in such a primitive fashion. Sir Aeneas wrote that 'being very agreeable in conversation and of an insinuating address she persuaded 700 of the clan to take up arms in the Steuart cause under the command of McGillevray of Dunmaglass, chief of Clan Vick Gillevray with a sufficient number of Commission and Noncommission officers'.

A list of the names of the officers is very revealing. The Lieutenant-Colonel was described as 'merchant of Inverness', two officers as 'tacksmen' and three as 'farmers', three came from the Laich of Moray (Petty and Cantray) and most of the others from Strath Nairn. Only three came from Moy, Fraser, the smith, a servant and Gillies Macbean, a younger son from a Strath Nairn family, who is described as 'a brewer'. He lived at Dalmagarry and was probably the innkeeper. They appear to be the only names from Strathdearn and there is only one from Badenoch. Although the pedigrees of several of the local farmers go back to the eighteenth century, none of them had a tradition that forebears had been 'out' in the '45. In those days the country magnates were, socially, more closely associated with the society of the nearest town. This comes out very strongly in Sir Aeneas' *Notes*. Many still had their winter houses there instead of going to Edinburgh or London. Lady Mackintosh herself was to receive a signal honour from the burgh of Inverness in later years. The names of a few members of the Clan Chattan Association that I have mentioned show how strong were the clan associations within the town. As Mr R. McGillivray points out the regiment was officered by very young men.[26] One can fairly deduce that the composition of her regiment was not founded upon the structure of the clan, as had been the case in the Mackintosh regiment of the '15, but upon her social charm and friendship and upon the strong anti-English and anti-union feeling of the period.

There does not seem to be any record of where the new regiment was embodied but it joined Prince Charles Edward's army on its return from Derby and was present at the Battle of Falkirk where it occupied a position in the centre of the front line and did well.

After the Battle of Falkirk the Prince's army marched north via Perth to Blair Atholl. The Highland troops then marched through the hills by Drumochter to Badenoch. The first objective was to reduce the forts held by Government troops at Fort Augustus and other places and to dispel the army stationed at Inverness under the command of Lord Loudon. It was also hoped to ease the problem of a very deficient commissariat by allowing some of the soldiers to winter at home.

Lord Loudon's army of about 1700 men consisted mainly of the Independent Companies which had been raised by those Highland chiefs who supported the Government. The chiefs had the privilege of choosing their officers and the chance of a paid job was an enormous attraction to the poverty-stricken Highlanders, crowded as they were upon their unproductive land and with minimal opportunities to better themselves. Mackintosh was actually in Inverness with Loudon's army. On Sunday, the 16th February, while the main Jacobite forces were still in Badenoch, the Prince came to stay at Moy Hall. He was accompanied by a comparatively small guard of Camerons and Macdonalds of Clan Ranald. Lady Mackintosh of course made him welcome. She entertained him to a supper that 'was exceedingly genteel and plentiful'.

There are several accounts of the stirring events of the night that followed. Allan Maclean gives a good summary of them in the *Clan Chattan Journal* (Vol. 7, No. 3, pp. 129-32). But to me the story of the affair has a live interest because I heard it, as told locally, by the great-grandson of Donald Fraser the blacksmith of Moy, the famous 'Captain of the Five'. I always picture his ancestor as looking like him, an extremely handsome man with so much presence that, in a district where most men were referred to as Alec this or Donnie that, he was always spoken of as Mr Fraser.

According to the local version as I was told it, word came to Lady Mackintosh that Lord Loudon, hearing that the Prince was staying at Moy, planned a night attack to capture him. She sent for Donald Fraser, the blacksmith, as the best man she could turn to in this emergency. He, with four other men, went to watch the road from Inverness. When they heard Loudon's troops coming, they took up a position where the road debouches from the narrow Stairsneach nan Gaidheal, taking cover behind peat stacks and calling to one another as if they were the different clans in the Prince's army, and firing their guns. In the darkness, the looming peat stacks gave the impression that a large force of men was

The late Donald Fraser, the great-great-grandson of Donald Fraser, 'The Captain of the Five', with his wife and son, John.

there waiting to attack the column of Government troops as it issued from the pass. It is certainly true that Loudon's men panicked. This local account rather vaguely stated that information that Loudon was planning his night attack was brought by a boy who had been sent by a servant who had been waiting at table and had overheard Loudon's officers discussing the operation.

It has been pointed out that peat stacks would not normally be left standing till February, but my grandfather, speaking of Strath Spey, said that his great-uncle was a child in 1745 and that he was specially told to notice (and remembers seeing) the stooks of corn still standing in the fields on New Year's Day because the harvest had been abnormally bad and so many men were in the Grant company in Loudon's Army. Things must have been even less normal in Strathdearn. The panic of the whole force, given as 1500 men, was true enough according to all the accounts, although the only casualty was Macleod's piper, Donald Ban MacCrimmon who, according to tradition, had had a premonition of his death and had composed his own lament – the well-known '*Cha Till MacCriomain*' ('MacCrimmon Will Not Return'). The troops were so demoralized, and the accounts of strong Jacobite forces ready to attack were so circumstantial, that Loudon at once made plans for evacuating Inverness and retreating into Ross-shire.

According to another account news of the intended expedition had reached old Lady Mackintosh, the widow of the 20th Chief, who was living in Inverness, and she sent off a lad to Moy to give warning of it. As Loudon had ordered all the roads from the town to be guarded, the lad had to be smuggled out of the town under the cape of a dragoon and only reached Moy not long before the expedition would have got there – if Donald Fraser had not routed it.

Bishop Forbes in *The Lyon in Mourning* states that Captain Macleod (Donald Macleod of Galtrigill who guided the Prince on his perilous journey to the Outer Isles) told him that the Prince had told him the Laird of Mackintosh himself was the kind friend who had sent off the express from Inverness to give notice of the danger. The Prince said he had a 'very good opinion of that gentleman'.[27] One wonders whether the Laird gave this rather belated warning or if it had been in response to a much earlier direct message from him that Anne Mackintosh sent Donald Fraser to watch the road. If so she kept the warning to herself.

After the elegant supper at Moy Hall the royal guest retired and, when the lad arrived with the warning that Loudon's men were actually on their way, he had to be roused from heavy sleep and there was evidently much confusion. Allan MacLean quotes a contemporary account: 'In the close (i.e. the courtyard) the writer saw the Prince walking with his bonnet above his nightcap and his shoes down in the heels; and Lady Mackintosh in her smock petticoat running through the close, speaking loudly and expressing her anxiety about the Prince's safety.' He was escorted some two miles down the loch and Lady Mackintosh hid in the garrets the valuables from the Prince's room and sent his baggage wagons to a place of hiding in the woods.[28]

Donald Fraser, the blacksmith of Moy, described as 'a trusty stout fellow' was made an officer in the Mackintosh regiment and was ever after known as '*Caiptin nan Coig*' ('Captain of the Five'). He fought at Culloden and survived. He then considered it safer to leave Moy and move to somewhere near the Slochd. But he is buried in Moy church-yard and his fine tombstone, of a very beautiful marble, was sent from Rome by Jacobite admirers there.

On Tuesday, the 18th February, the Prince's army marched along the road from Badenoch to Moy on its way to Inverness. Just before one comes to Moy school house, on a little hillock on the opposite side of the road, there is a stone with two grooves in it crossing each other. It is said they were made by the soldiers sharpening their swords 'on their way to Culloden' and that it was possible to pick up flints dropped from their flintlock guns. I was never so lucky.

To contradict the ridiculous stories that 'Colonel Anne' personally led her regiment into battle, Sir Aeneas was at pains to note that she 'never saw the men but once and was at her own house the time of the action' (i.e. the Battle of Culloden). It was probably on this march that she saw them and a tradesman's account of about this time records entries of the purchase of quantities of white ribbon. It is tempting to picture her making this into white cockades with which to decorate her regiment and that she presented these badges as they came to Moy on this march.

The Prince pressed on to Inverness 'one end of which he entered at the time his Lordship [Loudon] quitted the other'. The last of Loudon's army was actually embarking to cross the Firth to Ross-shire. The Prince made Inverness his headquarters for about two months, staying in the house of the dowager Lady Mackintosh. He sent detachments to capture Fort Augustus and into Ross-shire in pursuit of Loudon's army. The Mackintosh regiment was with this second force. They dispersed Loudon's army and a party of them bumped into some of Loudon's troups near Dornoch. About sixty prisoners were taken including Mackintosh himself. It must have been an embarrassing moment for all concerned but the Prince, with perfect tact, sent him to his wife writing that he 'could not be in better security or more honourably treated'. For how long he stayed at Moy or where he went afterwards one longs to know.

This string of random recollections evoked by the road is not the place to describe the Battle of Culloden. But, as the sound of the firing is said to have been heard at Moy Hall, and as it was along this road the Jacobite army had marched north so proudly only two months before, and as back along it some of the poor broken fragments were to seek safety, it is inevitable that I should mention it.

While the Prince and his army had been in occupation of Inverness, the Government army, under the command of the Duke of Cumberland, had been moving up the east coast. On the way Cumberland had specially trained his men in methods of meeting the deadly Highland charge. On the 14th April news came to the Prince that Cumberland had crossed the Spey. That formidable obstacle had not been defended and the Prince prepared to give him battle within a few miles of Inverness. There has been much controversy as to who was to blame for many mistakes. A bare outline of events as they affected the Mackintosh regiment is as follows.

On the 15th April the Jacobite army took up a position on Culloden Moor, which was then open moorland. It was a place where Cumberland could make use of his great superiority in artillery and cavalry and which did not afford the Highlanders the sort of ground suitable for their special mode of fighting – the very kind of ground available in the hills just across the Nairn.

The Jacobite army was greatly below its possible strength because of poor commissariat arrangements. Many of the best troops, including the Macphersons, had not rejoined it after being sent home for the winter in order to save their keep. Supplies of food were so inadequate that many of the men had gone to Inverness to try to obtain some. The only food provided for those who remained was one biscuit per man for that day, the night march that followed and the battle the next day. The full strength of the army should have been 6000 men but at the battle it only numbered about 5000. Cumberland, on the other hand, had 9000 troops in good condition. As Sir Aeneas pointed out, it was a seasoned army opposed to a force made up of militia. In cavalry and artillery it was infinitely superior.

Cumberland on his march halted at a place not far from Nairn. As the Jacobite leaders learnt that it was his birthday they decided to make a night attack in order to surprise his army after its celebrations. This plan miscarried, the march took longer than had been calculated, and the army only reached Cumberland's camp shortly before dawn; it was decided to return to Culloden. Various reasons have been given for this fiasco. It seems a pity that those officers in the Mackintosh regiment, who came from Petty and knew the district intimately, had not been consulted and used as guides.

Back on Culloden Moor, wearied from the night march and almost without food, the Jacobite army awaited the attack of the larger, better equipped Hanoverian forces who were rested and in good condition. The Highlanders, who formed the main force in the army, were drawn up in the front line. The Mackintosh regiment was in the centre. By idiotic mismanagement the three Macdonald regiments had been placed on the left and the men of this important section of the army were mortally offended. It was almost equally unfortunate that the right end of the line rested on a dry stone dyke which was to prove a most deceptive protection from a flank attack. As they waited, a bitter east wind blew icy showers of sleet into their faces.

Cumberland, to counter the effect of a Highland charge such as had broken Mackay's line at Killiecrankie, had placed his infantry in two lines, each line consisting of three ranks and the second line so far behind the first one that there was a field of fire should the Highlanders break through. He had placed some of his artillery at intervals in his first line.

The battle started about 1pm with an artillery duel in which Cumberland's army had a very great superiority and casualties among the Highlanders, in the front line who were exposed to it, were very heavy. By gross ineptitude they were exposed to this in total inaction for about half an hour. At last, galled beyond endurance, the Mackintosh regiment charged and all the rest of the front line joined them except the Macdonalds, who stood in sullen immobility and allowed themselves to be shot down as they stood. Finally, they were marched off the field.

As the Highlanders came, Cumberland's front line opened fire and the guns changed to grape shot. The Highland losses were terrible, their dead bodies fell one on top of the other, but they continued their headlong charge and struck the front line of the enemy with such impact that they broke it in several places. The Mackintoshes continued their charge across the fatal space, between the two lines of Government troops, and were mown down by the concentrated fire of the second line. They continued their rush towards the enemy. Only one man in the whole Highland charge actually reached Cumberland's second line and he fell dead as he did so.

The charge was so sudden that it received no support and nothing was done to bring the Jacobite second line into action. At the same time some of Cumberland's men (the Campbell regiment) had come round the other side of the dry stone dyke on the Jacobite right and used it as cover from which to fire. They then pulled it down to let the Dragoons through to attack the survivors of the Jacobite charge and break up the remaining units. The main part of the battle is said to have lasted little more than forty minutes, by one account even less, and of this a comparatively short time was spent in actual fighting.

The losses of the Mackintosh regiment were particularly heavy. Out of 700 men and twenty-one officers only 300 men and eight officers survived.[29] John Roy Stewart, the Strath Spey soldier and poet, wrote in his 'Day of Culloden':

> Redoubled are shed my tears for the dead,
> As I think of Clan Chattan the foremost in fight;
> O woe for the time that has shrivelled their prime,
> And woe that the left had not stood at the right.

They took, however, a heavy toll of the enemy. The total loss in Cumberland's army amounted to 300 men dead and injured and of these many were in the two regiments exposed to the Highland charge.

In the pursuit that followed the defeat some of the broken units of the Jacobite army fled towards Inverness right up to the outskirts of the town. I have been told of one place said to be haunted by men cut down by the pursuing dragoons. A number, however, were able to make for the hills to their right. The normal way would be by Daviot from which a track ran across Strath Nairn and into Strathdearn by the same line as that taken by the Parliamentary bit of our road. Sir Aeneas wrote that 'several of Charles' adherents past the house in their shirt sleeves in a bloody condition and panting for want of Refreshment'.[30] Lord George Murray rallied a considerable part of the shattered army and retreated by the same route. In the Orders for the Day to Prince Charles's army, which started with much formality and detail, the last pathetically brief entries are: 'Wednesday 16th Aprile, battle, and retired to Currybroch, 17th to Balnahespich, by Aviemore, Strathspey, 18th to Ruthven of Badenoch where Army dispersed *inde* to Glen Fisshy in Badenoch *sub dio*.'[31]

In other words they put the Findhorn as well as the Nairn behind them, before they halted for the night, and then they crossed the Spey and spent the second night on the further side of Loch Inch at the old Balnespick (from which the Strathdearn one takes its name). Then they went not to the ruined barracks opposite Kingussie but to another Ruthven at the head of Badenoch.

It is fortunately unnecessary to dwell on the disgraceful behaviour of the Government forces after Culloden, of the deliberate murder of the wounded and, at a higher level, of the imprisonment under atrocious conditions, transportations and executions.

Strathdearn suffered from the parties that were sent out to search for arms and destroy the implements of husbandry. A letter in the 'Seafield Papers', from Sir Archibald Grant of Monymusk, dated 23 April 1746 details the capture by such a party of thirty-six guns, ten swords, eight bayonets, one pistol, thirteen culters of ploughs and fourteen socks of ploughs. One party that came to Strathdearn drove off the cattle, killed men and women and burnt down part of the newly built inn at Dalmagarry. It must have been from this party that some men came to Moy Hall, as Sir Aeneas so vividly described, and enquired of Lady Mackintosh herself 'for that damd Rebell Lady McIntosh'. Sir Aeneas goes on to tell how Mr Lesly, the minister, seeing the soldiers approaching the house, forded the river in a hurry

thinking by his presence to prevent the men from committing any atrocities. But he might just as well have not come. Accidentally pulling out his watch, it was snatched from his hand in a moment. Lady McIntosh pitying the good man offered a guinea to the soldier for it, the soldier called out 'Damit, you have got money' and immediately took her purse in which was fifty guineas which was all she possessed. A second soldier insisted that she had more money, and upon her declaring in the negative he very cruelly with his bayonett struck her on the breast; luckily it only grazed upon the Bone. There is no saying what the wretch might have done had not a Soldier at that Instant seized him by the Collar and told him, that if he used any further insult to that Lady, that he would stab him. It was afterwards discovered that the Lady had saved the latter from being flogged at Perth. Sr Everet [Falconer], secretary to Cumberland, about this time, arriving with the Troups, the Stragglers disappeared. Sr Everet, who had been an Admirer of the Lady, recollecting her face cried out 'My God do I see Miss Farquharson whom I so much loved.' He did all he could to discover the soldiers who had behaved so badly; but she begged that no further Enquiry might be made. She then, being mounted on a thorough bred horse, the only one left and which belonged to her husband, proceeded for Inverness, it happened to be at retreat beating when they arrived near the Duke's Camp close upon the Town when the horse pricking up his Ears carried her to where the Drummers were. 'Oh dam it' cried the Soldiers 'this is surely the horse she charged upon in the Battle'.

A gentleman in the Scots army saw her being brought in. He described her as 'a woman of a masculine spirit, who raised the clan of that name notwithstanding her husband was in Lord Loudon's army. She behaved quite undaunted and with great unconcern. She said we had made a sad slaughter of her regiment, for that all her officers were killed except three.'

Sir Aeneas goes on to say that Lady Mackintosh was imprisoned, apparently in some house in Inverness, and

> confined to her room for six weeks at the expiration of which she was set at liberty nothing appearing against her and her friends having great Interest. During her confinement the Commissary of Provisions had orders to furnish her with what quantity of Bread she required, frequently 12 loaves in a day, which was the means of saving the lives of many poor wretches confined in the prisons for wrong principles.

Lady Mackintosh, having been arrested, a party of men, whom Sir Aeneas is very tactful in describing as an 'inimical clan', seized the opportunity of settling old scores with Mackintosh. Their leader was in fact Alexander Grant of Dalrachnie. He was a kinsman of Sir Alexander Grant of Dalvey and he had obtained a wadset of the farm of Inverlaidnan. It was there that the Prince had stayed the night before he came to Moy, no doubt much against Grant's will for he strongly supported the Government. It is thought that it was he who sent word to Loudon that the Prince would be staying at Moy Hall with a small escort; his mother refused to bake bread for the Prince's party on the excuse that it was the Sabbath. Sir Aeneas's tact in describing the episode that followed is all the more amusing to read because Dalrachnie was his connection by marriage, his own wife being a Grant of Dalvey.

Inverlaidnan was a very good farm and Dalrachnie's lands stretched across the valley of the Dulnain just beyond the modern village of Carrbridge and to Forrigin on the slope below the Slochd. He was the Baron Bailie of the Regality of Grant. This was a more important office than that of the factor (and, as a matter of fact, two of his sons were successively factors of the great Grant estates). Sir Ludovic, at that time the Laird of Grant, lived in London, and Dalrachnie was said to be the most powerful man in Strath Spey. In addition he probably had a good deal to do with the management of two estates in Strathdearn itself, Raigmore and Clune, which his kinsman Sir Alexander Grant of Dalvey, who was mainly concerned with business affairs in London, had just bought. (The finest of these lands, Raigmore and Clune were soon afterwards sold by Dalvey to my mother's great-grandfather.) One can well imagine that there would be rivalry between a hard-up aristocrat, as was Mackintosh of Mackintosh, and a man who, although of gentle birth, would have seemed to him a *parvenu*, but there is no record of any particular quarrel between them.

Grant of Dalrachnie was an officer in the force of men, under the command of Sir Archibald Grant of Monymusk, who were employed in collecting arms and reducing the area of Strath Spey and Strathdearn to obedience. Perhaps on the instigation of Dalrachnie, Sir Archibald visited Moy Hall to investigate reports 'that there are valuable things in the Island and some people there guarding it, and that they have a boat in the Island'. Not having means of reaching the island Sir Archibald had sentries placed all round the loch.[32]

Sir Archibald seems then to have allowed Dalrachnie to take control. According to Sir Aeneas it was he who, having obtained access to the island, carried off all the swords and the ancient weapons that were heirlooms. Hearing of this Mackintosh who, according to Sir Aeneas, 'was in Inverness' (but where was he and what was he doing during the Battle of Culloden?!) approached Cumberland through Loudon and represented 'that these arms had never been employ'd against Government, but had been in the family ages before'. The Duke, upon Loudon's report, taking up the sword which had been received from King Charles I, said, 'I suppose this is the sword his Lady used in her expeditions', and instantly gave orders for their being returned!

Grant of Dalrachnie worked further mischief. One may uncharitably suspect that he had started the rumours that led to the expedition to the island in order to destroy or secure certain papers. It must be remembered that in those days, in the Highlands, financial transactions were largely done by means of bonds, obligations and quittances and Mackintosh and he, as near neighbours, may well have had business dealings with each other. In any case the family papers, as well as the arms, had been removed from the island where they had been placed for safety and taken back to the house where 'the inimicable clan read and burnt several of consequence to the family'. One would give anything to know what Dalrachnie was looking for and if he found it. Mackintosh, hearing of what was going on, 'obtained from Cumberland a force of 200 men to protect his property. He went to Moy and, on entering the dining-room, found his papers scattered through the room. He showed Dalrachnie his orders and said, 'that if he and his men did not turn out instantly, he would make use of the power in his hands'. This 'had the desired effect and they disappeared'. It is satisfactory to know that the intruder, in this episode, did not prosper. Alexander Grant of Dalrachnie's position soon deteriorated. With the passing of the Act abolishing the Heritable Jurisdictions, the Regality of Grant and, with it, its office of Baron Bailie came to an end and Sir Ludovic's successor, the 'good Sir James', redeemed the wadset of Inverlaidnan.[33]

With this satisfactory outcome for Mackintosh, the story of the actual participation of Moy in the history of the '45 comes to an end. It is interesting to estimate how much Strathdearn was affected by the series of Acts of Parliament that, in great haste, were passed to make a further rising impossible.

To curb the powers of the chiefs and Highland land-owners an Act abolishing Heritable Jurisdictions was passed but the only rights under this Act that Mackintosh had, and for which he claimed compensation, were over lands in Lochaber where he had hardly ever been able to exercise them. He got nothing.

The tenure of Ward Holding, i.e. the obligation of a vassal to render military service to his feudal lord was abolished. This obligation had clearly become burdensome and had, on occasion, been overridden by the yet greater claims of clanship. Undoubtedly this Act deeply affected the relationship between a great many landowners and their tenants and contributed to 'the Clearances'. But as one goes along this bit of the road one finds evidence of a more gradual and most beneficial change: the advancement from the need of 'manpower' to defend the clan and support the chief and landlord, tending to lead to gross overcrowding, to the normal relationship of laird and tenant farmer. This change came about in wide areas of the Highlands but in Strathdearn, one man, Sir Aeneas Mackintosh, was largely responsible for bringing it about.

By yet a third Act the wearing of Highland Dress was prohibited. Under this Act 'no man or boy within that part of Great Britain called Scotland, other than such as shall be employed as Officers and Soldiers in His Majesties Forces shall, on any pretext whatsoever, wear or put on the clothes commonly called the Highland clothes (that is to say) the Plaid, Philabeg, little Kilt, Trowse, Shoulder-belts or any part whatsoever of what peculiarly belongs to the Highland Garb', or if any person were found wearing a dress composed of tartan or parti coloured cloth he should be imprisoned six months without option of bail for the first offence and on its repetition be transported for seven years. Highlanders were made to swear, as they would answer at the Day of Judgement, that they possessed no articles of Highland dress and that, if they did so, might they be accursed in their undertakings, family and property, be killed in battle as a coward and be buried in a foreign land without Christian burial.[34] It is difficult to estimate how widely this Act was enforced. From general reading I am under the impression that it was mainly used as a convenient excuse for making politically desirable arrests. There is no record of a prosecution either for wearing Highland dress or for carrying arms (which was prohibited under another Act) in Strathdearn but it must have come into force there, for Sir Aeneas, generally so good-natured in his comments, is scathing about its effects: 'Since deprived of their Dress, much of the ancient spirit has left the Commons and you now see them lounging in a Great Coat and affraid to wet their feet.' The wearing of Highland dress and the use of guns, however, certainly continued, or was soon resumed, as is obvious in Robertson's account of the wedding at the Coigs and from the two Statistical Accounts.

There was no general aftermath of bitterness after the '45. In fact there was soon a wave of Jacobite sensibility in fashionable circles. Flora Macdonald was lionized after her release and Sir Aeneas writes:

In the year 1748 Lady Mackintosh being at London was carressed by Ladys of Quality of the same way of thinking, was very intimate in the Prince of Wales' family and so favourably received by the publick that she never met with any Insult on account of her principles. Allan

Ramsey, the fam'd Scots painter took a likeness of her, thousand copys of which were bought in a short time.

A.M. Mackintosh in a footnote (pp. 349-50) quotes a story that the Duke of Cumberland gave a ball that was attended by Lady Mackintosh. The first tune played was called, 'Up and waur them a' Willie' and the Duke asked her to dance it with him. She complied and then asked him whether, as she had danced to his tune, he would dance to one of her choosing. 'A great gallant he could not refuse' and she called for a tune, 'The auld Stuarts back again'. Remembering the excesses of Butcher Cumberland it seems to me an extraordinary example of the insensitivity of that class-bound and elegant age.

One wonders still more how she and her husband got on together. Sir Aeneas, writing of her release from imprisonment, added: 'Several who pretended friends on this occasion did everything in their power to hurt her, but finding she rose superior to their malice began again to cringe to her, and she had the greatness of soul to forgive them.' Of course Mackintosh may in the background have done his best to help and protect her, but no activity, such as he showed in protecting his property against Dalrachnie, is recorded. One just wonders if Sir Aeneas, so tactful about all that concerned the Rising, evidently so full of admiration for her and so circumspect in his allusions to his uncle, meant more than he wrote. Mackintosh and his wife apparently lived together at Moy for the remaining twenty-four years of his life but the house, where so much had happened, was accidentally burnt down and so one cannot even picture the setting of their lives.

After the publicity attending 'Colonel Anne's' success in raising a regiment to fight for the Prince it must have given Mackintosh considerable pleasure to know that, in spite of the losses at Culloden, in 1754 he himself was able to recruit 500 men to serve in the 42nd (Black Watch). 'At his funeral 1500 men without arms were present.'

In 1763 she received the unique honour of being elected 'burgess free-woman and guild sister of the Burgh of Inverness'. He died in 1770. She outlived him for fourteen years and died in Edinburgh. She was buried in Leith with her own family.

Sir Aeneas

There have been a great many Chiefs of Clan Mackintosh but so little is known about them that most of them are no more than names and numbers to us. There is scope at least for imagining that William (7th), with his strange request that he should be buried on an island in Loch Arkaig, was appreciative of the value of property, or that Malcolm (10th) who routed the Comyns, was a bonnie fechter, and that Lachlan (19th), who affronted Coll Macdonald of Keppoch and had to be pressurized into accepting terms of peace with the Camerons, was, in Sir Aeneas Macpherson's words, 'arrogant'. Angus (22nd), the husband of 'Colonel Anne', remains something of an enigma.

In the case of his successor, Angus, classicalized into Aeneas, or more colloquially Eneas, it is very different. We know more about him and through his *Notes Descriptive and Historical, Principally Relating to the Parish of Moy in Strathdearn*, we have the great privilege of seeing Strathdearn through the eyes of a very observant man of the eighteenth century. Again and again in these recollections prompted by the road, I have quoted from his *Notes*. He was, however, very much more important than as an amiable collector of social data and it is fitting that he should be commemorated by the obelisk on the island in Loch Moy. In fact, when one considers the role he played during a most trying time in the history of the Highlands, one feels that probably he was the most influential man in the long list of Mackintoshes of Mackintosh.

The outline of the story of his life is simply told. He succeeded his uncle as Chief and so 'Colonel Anne' was his aunt by marriage. He must have spent a large part of his youth at Moy for he states that he attended the village school there. He succeeded Angus (22nd) in 1770. When the American War of Independence broke out he lost no time in raising a company to serve in the 2nd Battalion of Fraser's Highlanders, afterwards known as the 71st. (This was later disbanded and has no connection with the present 71st Regiment — the Highland Light Infantry.) He sailed for America in 1776 and had an adventurous voyage for the ship was attacked by privateers. He saw much active service in 1777-81 and when Lord Cornwallis capitulated he became a prisoner-of-war and did not return to Scotland until 1783. In his *Notes* he never mentions his own exploits. He married in 1785 a daughter of Sir Ludovic Grant of Dalvey but he had no children. In 1800 the house that had seen so much history was accidentally burnt down and he built a new one. In 1812 he was created a baronet and he died in 1820.[35] He was succeeded by his nearest male heir, a third cousin — his great-grandfather's great-great-grandson.

Sir Aeneas Mackintosh of Mackintosh (23rd Chief).

His importance lies in the example that he gave and the influence that he exerted during the period of social disorientation that followed the Risings of the '15 and the '45 and the effects of the Abolition of Heritable Jurisdictions and of Ward Holding – the measures that the Government took to make a repetition of such Risings impossible. It was no longer possible to call out a following of armed men and, as law and order were at last being maintained efficiently in the Highlands, this was no longer necessary. About the same time the discovery was made that the hardy black-faced sheep could thrive on the Highland hills. Wool was in great demand. The Highland gentry increasingly came into contact with the higher living standards of the South and, in many cases, the rents of their lands, the income upon which they depended, were in arrears. In all too many cases they yielded to the temptation to sell or let their land to flock-masters and 'the Clearances' began. All this happened at a time when society had been rent by civil war and when the Highlanders had been humiliated by the abominable behaviour of the Government and its agents.

That the situation did not degenerate into a confrontation between the victors and the vanquished, between the haves and the have-nots, into an insoluble problem such as that in Northern Ireland and all too many other places, past and present, is largely due to the sanity, the benevolence and the wisdom of a group of individuals to whom enough credit is never given. These were three great landowners: the Dukes of Argyll and of Gordon and Sir James Grant of Grant; there were many more, with less land, such as MacDougall of MacDougall and the Laird of Colonsay. Some had consistently supported the Government like Argyll. The policy of the Gordon family had changed. The MacDougalls of MacDougall had been Jacobite. They all accepted the new social conditions and were loyal subjects of the Government. They were all distinguished by a determination to improve the old inefficient methods of farming and to raise the condition of the country people from utter poverty.

Sir Aeneas was not a great agriculturalist but, like these others, he did pre-eminent service in helping to heal the wounds of the past and in adjusting society to the changes of the present. He had proved his own loyalty by his active service in America but he roundly condemned Cumberland and his subordinates after Culloden. He could write,

to speak impartially the consequences that have followed the

Suppression of the Rebellion have been of the utmost consequence to the Highlands of Scotland, by abolishing the Jurisdiction Act which kept the dependents of Great Families in a most abject state, the introduction of Manufactorys and Industry into it, the opening of Communications through the Country by improving the Roads and Taverns, and in short, in civilizing the inhabitants by admitting Strangers among them.[36]

Nevertheless he gloried in the long history of his family and his clan. He had a deep appreciation of the courage and idealism of the Jacobites. Sometimes his sentiments become a little mixed. In describing the Battle of Culloden, which he termed 'a day fatal to the guilded hopes of the deluded Steuarts', he proudly tells of the clansman who, when the standard bearer was killed, held it up and then saved it by wrapping it round his body. He relates with obvious relish that, after being subjected to the protracted bombardment, the Highlanders 'disliking this distant mode of fighting, advanced with great bravery to the right of the Royal Army where Monro and Barrell's Regiment were posted, and when near, gave a fire, threw down their firelocks and fell into the heart of these Regiments, sword in hand, and soon broke them'.

He did not try, unlike most of the benevolent landowners of his day, to change his tenants' way of living. He describes the cluster of houses of the eight joint tenants of the farm of Moy More as a village and, in an amusing anachronism, adds that they could frequently turn out twenty men capable of bearing arms. He admits that, although the soil is good, owing to bad management in cold winters it did not furnish enough corn to feed the inhabitants. He was, however, deeply conscious of the responsibilities of a proprietor. After scathing criticism of those who, 'through their attention to the Art of Agriculture make improvements that displace "the poor harmless hind" from the few acres upon which his family depended', he adds, 'Happy the Man whose tenants look upon him as their father, and follow his advice as children, who in their distress, whether of Body or Circumstances, administers Relief unasked ...' He lived up to his word. The inscription on his monument reads: 'His paternal Regard to his Tenants displayed itself in a spontaneous remission of a third part of their Rents During the general Distress which prevailed in the last years of his life'. To do the lairds justice, the Parliamentary Report upon the famine of 1845, and earlier famines, shows how general and generous was the help given by many

Highland landlords, hard hit as they themselves often were by the failure of the harvest. Moy More and the other farms on the Mackintosh estate have, for a long time, been farmed by individual tenants using modern methods but the change came about gradually for it is still a saying in the countryside that Mackintosh never cleared a tenant from his land.

Sir Aeneas felt an equal sense of responsibility for the actual estate that he had inherited. He was childless but he cleared it of encumbrances and improved it. He strongly believed that descent should be by the male line and he drew up an elaborate entail to ensure this, thereby cutting out his own nephew (my great-grandfather).

It was in the same spirit that he wrote his *Notes*. One feels that what he recorded is just what he would have told his children if he had had any; and that he wrote down an account of the proud traditions of his family as a sacred bequest to the succeeding generations that he would never know. He notes the manpower, the possessions, the heraldry, the marriages, the cadet branches and many other details. He describes how the title, by which the Chief was known, altered as the lands that he occupied changed to 'of Connage', 'Dunachton' and 'Torcastle'. At the time he was writing it was 'Mackintosh of Mackintosh or Mackintosh of that Ilk. It is typical of the changed times that in the *Notes* he refers to himself as 'the laird'. It is noteworthy that he did not include the modern title of 'the Mackintosh'. This first appears in documents of the nineteenth century and in my young days, in old-fashioned families, it was used unwillingly. The old saying was quoted that there were only three 'thes' in Scotland – 'the Pope, the Devil and the Chisholm'. The custom of applying the definitive article to the head of the Chisholm family dates back to the Middle Ages when he was an incomer from the South and his name was adapted to the Gaelic as '*An Siosalach*'.

Sir Aeneas's *Notes* take the form of a description of the road from Castle Grant through Strathdearn, making a prolonged stop at Moy and on to Nairn with a description of the state of the countryside, the buildings, the manners, the customs and the stories. He expressed his delight at first catching a glimpse of Moy, 'that blessed spot', and of it he wrote:

Heaven has been very attentive to this place for in advanceing to and going from it, on all sides, the country is rough and barren, which serves as a background and setts off the whole to advantage; health resides in the peaceful vale and the cool limpid stream gushes from every rock, the heath cover'd mountains feed the bleating sheep and playfull kid, which furnish healthy meals to the swains, the honest ox and lowing sweet breathing cow, give flesh and milch to the sturdy Plow man, the air and water furnish wholesome food easily got at, shady groves are not wanting to indulge meditation, and every object round us makes the gratefull heart praise the Great Giver of Good for granting them.

His taste was that of the mid-eighteenth century, for sylvan charm rather than the stark grandeur of the high hills that the romantic age was to learn to appreciate. The low, wooded island set in the quiet waters of Loch Moy fulfilled his ideal of beauty. He loved the country for itself and not for sport. He evidently fished occasionally, but the otters, bred on the shores of the island, the roe deer, pastured with the cattle (which, in times of hunger came into the farmyard), and the black game roosted in the garden hedge, satisfied him more. His agriculture was old-fashioned; he sent his herd of cattle up to the shieling at Coignafearn. He made one planting of fir trees, where gentlemen of advanced years were allowed to shoot and ladies could go to watch them if they so wished, but he loved the native trees and bushes of the district, the birch, alder and hazel that feathered the slopes and water courses round Loch Moy.

A true patrician he was at ease in any company. He took for granted that divisions of class existed and he accepted his position with a strong sense of obligation. Of course, he spoke Gaelic but he did not write it. In his day even to speak it at school was taboo so that to read or write it must have been a difficult accomplishment to acquire. He was evidently on the closest and friendliest terms with the country people. He was also on very good terms with the townsfolk of Inverness. His account of the gay life lived there is rather amusing.

Inverness was very much more of a social centre in Sir Aeneas's time and he obviously was very fond of it. He writes: 'The amusements in winter are Assemblys once a fortnight, Card Meetings every day from 12 to 3 in the afternoon. Walking and Riding to the country, Concerts frequently, dancing every evening in private houses. The Gentlemen have fine Angling and Shooting, sometimes coursing.' The judges visited the town twice a year, at which times the ladies and gentlemen within fifty miles of the town repair to it. In the summer, a regiment was stationed there and there were frequent balls. 'Great Jollity' was kept up for six weeks at Christmas time 'when a dozen of families visit from

house to house and many a headach is the consequence'. He notes that
the ladies and gentlemen speak better English and are more easily understood in England than are the natives of any other town in Scotland. He
praises the complexions of the girls whom he says 'have a turn to musick
and dance rather well than gracefull in the opinion of strangers
unacquainted with Scots dances'. He notes how extremely well they can
mix with people of other places if they marry and leave the town and he
quotes a saying that, 'tho' they seldom bring fortunes they generally save
them to their husbands by their attention to his interests'.

'The Gentlemen having a turn of going abroad, generally run to the
Army or turn Merchants so that they mix the ideas of one country with
the other and make good Companions.' When they meet they 'naturally
converse on their different Adventures, the Bottle imperceptably goes
round, nor do they think of retiring till the wine gets the better' and
anyone who does so is considered to be a milk-sop. 'It is rather barbare
but such is the custom,' he adds.

He was hospitable. After praising the service at Dalmagarry Inn and
recommending the excellent claret at 2s. 6d. a bottle, I am sure that he
chuckled as he added that trade fell off when the family was in residence
at Moy Hall.

In reading his *Notes*, and recalling the green setting of the loch at Moy
which he loved so much, his presence is very real to one. It is not quite
that of his portrait which hangs at Moy Hall. That is very much a period
piece. There is no suggestion of a Highland association or of his way of
life as a countryman. It is of the figure of a typical gentleman of the
Georgian period, dressed in broadcloth and with an elaborate cravat. He
is comfortable but not portly and has great personal dignity. The most
striking feature in the face are the shrewd, deep-set eyes. Looking into
them one realizes that here is a man who could stand up to anyone and, to
everyone, was the kindest and best of company.

Moy As I Remember It

Sir Aeneas (23rd) died in 1820. One of his successors, Alexander (27th)
1861-75, made considerable additions to Moy Hall in the baronial style of
the period. The architect was, I think, Alexander Ross. The mid-
nineteenth century was a time when a great many board schools and
shooting lodges were being built. He is responsible for giving a Neo-
Gothic touch to the large number in the North that he designed. He also

is responsible for Inverness Cathedral, Skibo Castle and Aberlour Orphanage.

In 1875 Alexander was succeeded by his brother Alfred (28th). I was brought up in a family that cherished old fashions and looked rather askance at the indiscriminate use of the definite article 'the' as a title for a chief. Nevertheless the twenty-eighth Chief of Clan Mackintosh did indeed deserve a special designation. During his long chiefship he was most highly regarded by people in all ranks of society. He was Lord Lieutenant for Inverness-shire and Convener of Inverness County Council for thirty-five years. He took an active part in supporting the Cameron Highlanders (the County Regiment) and, finally, was appointed full Colonel of the Third Cameron Militia Regiment. He and Mrs Mackintosh of Mackintosh lived in great dignity for half of every year at Moy Hall, to which he made considerable additions in a very imposing style. His large establishment brought money and work to the district and formed a focus for its social life. One is apt to recall only the grandeur at Moy Hall but I also remember a derelict cottage just beyond the immaculately kept grounds. Mackintosh would not have it taken down because tramps liked to shelter there; it was known as 'Mackintosh's Hotel'. Unfortunately a careless tramp set it on fire one night and it was burned down.

The castellated style of the house encouraged people to believe that Prince Charles Edward had actually slept in it. But, although the old house had been accidentally burnt down, his bed had been religiously preserved. One visitor from the USA proudly announced that he thought that he had heard a ghost. The information was not well received. Mrs Mackintosh knew that, if such a rumour got about, most of the maids would give notice and she was *not* amused.

He was a keen sportsman. His estate contained eight grouse moors, three of them – Coignafearn, Meallmore and Moy – being among the best in the Highlands. The bags for the best seasons amounted to 4000 brace of grouse on Moy and over 2500 brace on each of the two others. He kept the shooting of Moy in his own hands. He was very skilful in the placing of the butts and the management of the drives and was an acknowledged authority on grouse shooting.

The shoots at which these great bags were achieved were very grand affairs and the house parties included the highest in the land. His Majesty, King George V, with Queen Mary, stayed at Moy several times and so did the future sovereign, His Royal Highness, the Duke of York, with his

Moy Hall. Royal Commission on the Ancient Monuments of Scotland.

Duchess. In 1921 the Prime Minister, Mr Lloyd George, was summoned to Moy Hall and a Cabinet Meeting was held in Inverness to discuss the Irish Treaty.[37] A royal visit to Moy Hall caused a flutter of pleased excitement throughout the district.

For a shy girl to visit Moy Hall, even at a far less august house party, was rather an awesome experience. As a matter of fact I was only there because a guest had failed and the party otherwise would have numbered thirteen. It was an experience to be waited on by footmen with powdered hair and silk stockings, and to eat off silver plates which I thought was much less nice than off china ones. It was easy to slip into a pleasant background where everyone was gracious and completely at ease. I found breakfast the most alarming of the meals, because there was no formality at it and one did not know where to sit. But it was a delicious meal with half-a-dozen side dishes to choose from and fresh home-baked breakfast rolls.

As a matter of fact the house party was a particularly interesting one because Cluny Macpherson and his wife were there and the old bitterness over the claim to the chieftainship of Clan Chattan had only lately been assuaged. But for me the party was more memorable because I met there, for the first time, Lady Cromartie, whose writing I greatly admired. Of course, she was not there as a very minor writer but as a leading social figure in the North (a countess in her own right, a great landowner and close relation of one of the most brilliant hostesses of London, the Duchess of Sutherland). She was enchanted to meet someone who esteemed her as the author of a few short stories. Very little of her work has been published but I wonder if this generation, which so much enjoys 'The Hobbit' and the 'Daleks' and half-believes in the 'Little Green Men', would not also like to enter the strange world of lordly, half-serpentine beings that was so real to her.

Another memory of Moy Hall is going with my mother to pay a call soon after the outbreak of the First World War. The footmen had been called up. Mrs Mackintosh was in agonizing anxiety about her only son and she was preparing to devote her energies to running a war hospital – but her immediate care was that she and her visitors should not be served with more than her ration of butter.

The twenty-eighth Chief of Mackintosh died in 1938 and the vast concourse at his funeral is still a local byword. Already since 1914 there had been great changes in the way of life at Moy Hall and there were more to come. During the Second World War the great house served

HM King George V and Mr Lloyd George as guests of Mackintosh of
Mackintosh at Moy Hall, 1911.

various war purposes and then stood empty for a time and finally was demolished. The present Mackintosh of Mackintosh and his family live in a house more suitable to modern ways of life. He does not call his clan to arms, as his predecessor did in the '15, and the stony islet in Loch Moy, where prisoners once awaited trial, is now permanently unoccupied. But he lives upon the oldest of his ancestral lands and he serves his people as their elected representative on the Regional Council. His clansmen, therefore, can count themselves very much more fortunate than those of a good many other clans.

8

Traffic on the Two Roads

From Moy to Stairsneach nan Gaidheal, the builders of the present, newest road follow much the same line as did General Wade in building the oldest road of all. Wade, himself, was taking the obvious, most direct route, across Strathdearn to the Slochd, that people must have used through the ages. The Grave of the Living Man, which is close to the road as it nears the Threshold, is a memorial of a very primitive way of life.

History was made upon this stretch of the old road. The Rout of Moy took place at this entrance to the Threshold and it was along this road that the Jacobite army marched so confidently to enter Inverness on the tail of Loudon's retreating forces. For me it revives the memory of a favourite story. The Reverend William Gordon, minister of Alvie, had defied Cumberland's orders to all local ministers to notify the authorities of Jacobite fugitives in their parishes and had, on the contrary, befriended them. This was reported to Cumberland. The minister was summoned to Inverness. I do not know if he walked or rode, or by what guard he was accompanied, but it is obvious that this would be the road he came by. and one may feel sure that, as he went, he wondered when, or if ever, he would take the same road home. When he was brought before the Butcher he addressed him, 'Your Royal Highness I am in great difficulty and I must ask your advice. My Heavenly King orders me to feed the hungry and help those in distress. My earthly King forbids me to do so. Which shall I obey?' Cumberland told him to obey his Heavenly King and to get out, and so he came back by the same road to a long and faithful ministry. His letters show that he was quite as capable of standing up to Sir Ludovic Grant of Grant as he was to the Duke of Cumberland and that he was the friend of Sir Ludovic's successor, the good Sir James, and helped him in plans for the benefit of Strath Spey.

Until the newest road was made this was the longest untouched stretch of Wade's road. For about ninety years it was part of the main road between Inverness and the South. Then a diversion was made further to the east following a line from Moy to the gap in the ridge of hills above Meallmore. This part of the road, made, and at first maintained, by the Parliamentary Commission for Highland Roads, continued to be the high road to Inverness until the making of the new road.

As I saw it, the old road wound like a crease in the heathery plain of Moy but in one's mind one peopled it with the folk who, coming and going, marked the enormous social changes of the period. There were still a number of drovers who disliked the hard surface for the hooves of their cattle. The great innovation that it brought about was the introduction of wheeled traffic into Strathdearn. The road itself was narrow. It was planned with little regard for the gradients of the contours and its surface was neither good nor well maintained. At one end of Strathdearn was the Slochd, at the other was the very steep pull into and out of Strath Nairn. In early days to drive along it was something of a pioneering effort. In 1740 Lord Lovat (Simon of the '45) travelled to Edinburgh in his coach. It took him eleven days. He very prudently took a wheel-wright with him, for he had a bad breakdown, but this occurred after he had safely crossed Strathdearn.[1] By 1809 a regular coach was running between Inverness and Perth. The journey took three days.[2]

In the Autumn, bands of reapers used to make their way down to the Lowlands. Corn was cut with the sickle and large bands of workers were needed to harvest it on the good farmlands of Fife and the Lothians. These were seasonal workers, but a great many people trudged south with little hope of returning. Some had lost their holdings, others of their free will had left their crowded glens to better themselves. A number went to work in the cotton mills that were being built to utilize Scotland's water power. New Lanark was, of course, a well-known and favourite example. Others entered the doomed hand-loom weaving industry. It is said that the porters of sedan chairs in Edinburgh were nearly all Highlanders. It was to meet the needs of these Highland immigrants that many of the Highland societies were founded. Material relief was given – the Highland Society of London founded orphanages that have survived to this day. They also worked to preserve the culture of the Gael. The Highland Society of Edinburgh has a specially good record for its services to piping and to the preservation of ancient Gaelic literature.

Wade's road itself was made for military purposes and had its associations with the Jacobite risings but, in my mind, it is also associated with the period of continuous fighting overseas between 1757 and 1815. This took place intermittently on the Continent beginning with the Seven Years' War, in America (first with the French then in the American War of Independence), in India against native rulers assisted by the French, in the West Indies, and at several points on the shores of the Mediterranean. It ended on the field of Waterloo. The battle honours of the Highland regiments bear witness to the gallant and decisive part that they played in all these areas of conflict.

One's own memories of Strathdearn during the two great wars of this century are largely connected with transport. One remembers how the railway line was guarded and, as civilians at home, our hearts went out to the trains going south because so many of them carried troops going to the Front. The road itself was constantly used by wheeled military traffic. As a motorist, one chafed behind the tail of many a long convoy of military lorries. The jeeps looked starkly functional compared to the sleek bodies of civilian cars. The formidable bulk of the armoured vehicles carried with them some realization of the terrors of war.

During the war period of the late-eighteenth and early-nineteenth century what little wheeled transport there was, was, of course, horse-drawn. The picture is mainly of marching men. But what a magnificent picture they must have made, when they were in full-dress uniform, in the days when the battle-dress of fighting men was not to make them invisible but to display them as formidably as possible. How splendidly the uniform of a Highland soldier of these days showed off his manly bearing. The fully trained and equipped troops, however, were mainly serving their country overseas. It is the endless gathering in of recruits, individually or in recruiting parties, along the Highland roads that make up one's mental picture.

A few Highland regiments had already been raised. The Black Watch, the 42nd in 1739, originally intended to keep law and order in the Highlands, the Independent Companies and Loudon's regiment, to counter the growing Jacobite menace, were disbanded in the aftermath of the '45 when the fighting qualities of the Highlanders were regarded as a liability, not an asset, to the security of the nation. Then Britain became involved in the Seven Years' War (1756), rivalry with the French intensified and spread further afield. At the beginning of the war period,

in 1757, William Pitt began his crusade to force the King and
Government to recognize the value of the Highlanders as soldiers and to
make use of them. In 1766 he made his famous speech upon the
triumphant justification of his efforts.

> I sought for merit wherever it was to be found, it is my boast that I was
> the first minister who looked for it and found it in the mountains of
> the North. I called it forth and drew into your service a hardy and
> intrepid race of men, who when left by your jealousy became a prey
> to the artifice of your enemies and had gone nigh to have overturned
> the State in the war before the last. These men in the last war were
> brought to combat on your side; they served with fidelity as they
> fought with valour and conquered for you in every part of the world.[3]

One of the earliest of the new Highland regiments to be embodied was
Fraser's Highlanders. It was raised by the son of that Simon Lord Lovat,
who was beheaded for his share in the '45. Young Fraser is said to have
raised 600 men from the Lovat Estates and 800 from the surrounding
district.[4] No doubt some of these men came from Strathdearn. Two other
regiments that were raised about this time, connected with the North-
East Highlands, were Montgomery's and Macleod's Highlanders. The
latter was not, as one would expect, based in Skye. Its name was changed
to that of the Highland Light Infantry. Fraser's Highlanders, after a few
years, were disbanded. This took place in Canada and the soldiers were
given grants of lands to settle there. But the habit of disbanding,
reforming and re-numbering regiments makes the complicated story of
the times even more difficult to follow.

When the American War of Independence began, Fraser's Highlanders
were again re-embodied and Sir Aeneas and 500 of his clansmen enlisted.
More and more Highland regiments from then onwards were formed.
Among them was the Strathspey Regiment, raised by Sir James Grant, the
Seaforth Highlanders (embodied in 1778) and the Cameron Highlanders
(embodied in 1793) the latter two having territorial associations with our
district. In all, to meet the growing emergency, about twenty-five
regiments were raised in the Highlands. Of these, five, including the
Seaforths and the Camerons, were retained upon a permanent footing.
All the others were disbanded or merged in other corps.[5] In addition,
from 1759 onwards, forty-two fencible regiments were raised in Scotland
for home defence. Twenty-six of these regiments were raised in the

Highlands. Though their terms of service were for home defence, the men generally showed a willingness to fill up the thinning ranks of regiments serving abroad.

A great many of the Highland regiments served in India and further opportunities for service were offered in the army raised by the East India Company. Military service in their local regiment with the East India Company, or in English regiments, offered a most welcome opportunity for a career to the younger sons of the gentry for whom it had become increasingly difficult to provide in the gross over-population of the Highlands. This one knows from family letters and traditions: to obtain 'a commission' was indeed a prize for many an active young man. Local men who served in India included members of the family of MacQueen of Corriebrough and of Mackintosh of Kyllachie. A member of a family that was becoming closely associated with Strathdearn was Eneas Mackintosh, son of my old forebear who farmed Dunachtan. Later in his career he served in the Cameron Highlanders, which he eventually commanded. He led the Forlorn Hope at the taking of Ciudad Rodrigo during the Peninsular War. In the battle tactics of the time, a Forlorn Hope was a small force sent to attack a fortress in order to reveal the disposition and strength of the defending forces. He survived this highly dangerous exploit and lies buried in the ruined chapel of St Ternan at Dunachton. My father's people in Strath Spey saw much service in India. Some of them rose to great distinction. Many of them died serving their country in the appallingly unhygienic conditions that then obtained in the East.

Fort George on the Moray Firth was in constant military occupation and Sir Aeneas remarked that a regiment was stationed at Inverness every summer for training. There must have been great military activity on the old road. Of those who served abroad, only too many did not return – casualties from illness and wounds were at an appallingly high rate in the days before Florence Nightingale. But fighting and hardship had been the lot of the Highlander for generations and some found splendid opportunities both in the New World and the East. For those who returned, both 'the Highland Lady' writing of Strath Spey and Sir Aeneas in his *Notes* on Strathdearn describe a life with many delightful aspects, in strong contrast to the gloomy accounts of conditions in many parts of the Highlands. For a few, there was the security of a pension and, leafing through old documents, it is pleasant now and then to come across the words 'Chelsea' or 'Chelseaman'.

I have never come across a serious attempt to estimate the effect of the Highland contribution to the war effort of the late-eighteenth and early-nineteenth centuries in bringing about the great change in the attitude of the public towards the Highlanders. No doubt, the romantic charm of Bonnie Prince Charlie and the writings of Sir Walter Scott, the 'Wizard of the North', also had a share in this. The wearing of the kilt had been made a criminal offence in the late 1740s. In 1822 it was not only donned by King George IV when he visited Edinburgh in state in that year but the Lord Mayor of London, who was a guest on that occasion, wore it as a compliment to Scotland. The kilt and the Highland bagpipe are now widely regarded as the national dress and musical instrument of Scotland. If one has read some of the descriptions of the Highlanders in the writings of Lowland historians from Fordoun onwards, and also the views expressed by members of the Scots Privy Council and King James VI and I, one can derive a good deal of amusement in imagining the utter disgust that these authorities would feel if they but knew.

Although there were a few unfortunate incidents when men were forced to enlist, on the whole the organization of the early Highland regiments, which was to some extent based on that of the clans, helped to soften the transition from one way of life to a totally different one. The Highland regiments have preserved the proper wearing of the kilt and prevented it from becoming a folksy survival. Great attention has preserved the highest standard of piping. Until 1854 there was no Government provision for regimental pipers. They were attached to each individual company and paid for by the officers. After 1854 they were 'put on the strength' and regimental pipe bands were formed; but to keep up the full number of pipers the officers still contribute. The range of music played has been extended from the playing of the highly stylized '*piobaireachd*', with a little dance music for diversion, to other kinds of music, notably regimental marches.

We Highlanders like to feel our roots, although most of us do not aspire to the ancient ancestry that the old seannachies made for some of us – we do not claim a descent from the royal line of Alba – like the McGregors; or from Conn of the 'Hundred Battles' – as do the Macdonalds; or, rather questionably, from the Fingalian hero, Diarmid O'Duin, like the Campbells. We cannot equal the Laird of MacNab who, according to the old story, when he was asked if his ancestors were of such antiquity that they shared the Ark with Noah, replied that the MacNabs had a boat of their own. Nothing warms the pride of our

Highland descent more than the sound of a rousing regimental march played by a pipe band. Our hearts throb with the rhythm of the roll of the drums. The plangent notes of the pipes stir our emotions. It does not matter that the addition of drummers to a pipe band is a felicitous introduction of the nineteenth century and that the marches – although some of their airs may be older – are contemporary with the regiments themselves. All things that are alive must change, adapt, adopt.

This stretch of Wade's road went out of use when the diversion through a gap in the hills to the eastward of the Stairsneach nan Gaidheal was made. Long before the making of this road, the gap in the hills would have been the most convenient route for the cattle from the Mackintosh lands in the Laich of Moray to be driven up to the shielings in Strathdearn in the summer migration. There must have been a great deal of coming and going between Moy and Petty, Connage and Rait. The gap was probably used by Coll Macdonald of Keppoch in his raid on Moy, and the men of the Mackintosh regiment, when they marched south to join the Rising of the '15, almost certainly came this way. We know that, after the Battle of Culloden, the remnants of the Jacobite army which Lord George Murray was able to rally, retreated by this gap. Fugitives from the shattered front line, where the men of Clan Chattan had fought, must surely also have sought safety by taking this well-known way. Many of them would have been wounded. Some of them would never have reached their homes. Jimmie Dunbar told me that, once when he was free-wheeling on his bicycle where the road slopes down to Moy, he suddenly saw a man in a plaid immediately in front of him. As he crammed on his brakes, the momentum of the bicycle carried him right through where the man had been and he felt and saw nothing. He stopped and looked back and he saw nothing.

This part of the road was made as part of a more comprehensive plan by the Government to relieve the poverty and unemployment in the Highlands, poverty that had been aggravated by the sudden changes following the collapse of the old social system. The road through Strathdearn was improved and maintained under the Parliamentary Commission for Highland Roads and by the fostering care of the two superintendents that they appointed, the two Mitchells, father and son. From the *Reminiscences* of Joseph Mitchell, the son, we have fascinating details as, for instance, that at first, commercial travellers used to ride carrying their samples in saddle-bags; later on they were able to drive in gigs with a good specimen of horseflesh between the shafts. The earliest stage coaches took three days to make the journey from Inverness to Perth. Then it was reduced to two days and, finally, the journey was made in one day, leaving Inverness at 5am and reaching Perth at 9pm.[6] Considering how much of the going was against the collar, this was a very good average. The coaches were well appointed and made a smart turn-out with good horses. One has come to associate stage coaches with Mr Pickwick and Sam Weller and the idea of one in full career across Strathdearn calls for some imagination.

When the railway was brought through Strath Spey a great deal of traffic was diverted from the road but, with the coming of the motor car, the balance was shifted again and the railway was little used. The road however, became blocked with traffic, including all too many lorries and caravans; so now the latest development in road construction, a new A9, has been almost completed to accommodate the increased traffic. Meanwhile, however, more and more aircraft, planes and helicopters, pass overhead and one wonders if a new era of transport is probably beginning. But whether it does or does not, the waters of the Findhorn will endlessly run their race to the sea as they did before a forgotten people left the foundations of their homes, the 'hut circles' in the wood above Inverbrough, or the Picts set up a stone beside the age-old track across Strathdearn and carved symbols upon it, the meaning of which has long since been lost and as they will continue their race when the sole surviving evidence of our existence in Strathdearn is probably the remains of the A9.

Notes

1 The Making of the Road

1. Sir Aeneas Mackintosh, *Notes Descriptive and Historical, Principally Relating to the Parish of Moy in Strathdearn*, Priv. printed, 1892, p. 14. Hereafter quoted as Sir Aeneas.
2. I am indebted to the Scottish Section of the Ordnance Survey and to Mr J.G. Dunbar of the Royal Commission on the Ancient Monuments of Scotland for their courtesy in giving me sections of maps.
3. Captain E. Burt, *Letters from a Gentleman in the North of Scotland*, 2 vols, Edinburgh, 1974, reprint of 1754 edn, Vol. 2, pp. 67-8. Hereafter quoted as Burt.
4. Bishop Robert Forbes, *Journals of the Episcopal Visitations of the Rt. Rev. Robert Forbes 1762 and 1770*, ed. J.B. Craven, London, 1886, p. 148.
5. J.B. Salmond, *Wade in Scotland*, 2nd edn, Edinburgh, 1938, p. 124.
6. A.M. Mackintosh, *The Mackintoshes and Clan Chattan*, Edinburgh, 1903, p. 325. Hereafter quoted as A.M. Mackintosh.
7. Sir Aeneas, p. 2.
8. Elizabeth Grant, *Memoirs of a Highland Lady*, London, 1928, p. 84.
9. George and Peter Anderson, *Guide to the Highlands and Islands of Scotland*, London, 1834, pp. 77-8.
10. *Aberdeen Journal*, 19 July 1773.
11. E. Grant, op. cit., p. 278.
12. A.R.B. Haldane, *New Ways through the Glens*, London, 1962, pp. 2-3.
13. O.S. Nock, *The Highland Railway*, London, 1973, pp. 3, 9-10.
14. Joseph Mitchell, *Reminiscences of My Life in the Highlands*, 2 vols, Newton Abbot, 1971, reprint of 1883-4 edn, Vol. 2, pp. 195-7. Hereafter quoted as Mitchell.
15. O.S. Nock, op. cit., p. 26.
16. H.A. Vallance, *The Highland Railway*, 3rd edn, Newton Abbot, 1969, p. 154.

2 Railway to River

1. Mitchell, Vol. I, p. 162.
2. G. Bain, *The River Findhorn from Source to Sea*, Nairn, 1911, p. 11. Hereafter quoted as Bain. Mr Murdo MacAskill has found remains of hut circles in the area.

3. For information on chambered tombs see A.S. Henshall's, *The Chambered Tombs of Scotland*, 2 vols, Edinburgh, 1963, 1972.

4. Sir Aeneas, p. 13.

5. William Forsyth, *In the Shadow of Cairngorm*, Inverness, 1900, p. 292. Hereafter quoted as Forsyth.

6. Bain, p. 47.

7. W.D. Simpson, *The Origins of Christianity in Aberdeenshire*, Aberdeen, 1925, pp. 8, 12, 14, 16, 33.

8. J.A. Duke, *The Columban Church*, Oxford, 1932, pp. 155-6.

9. *New Statistical Account of Scotland*, Edinburgh, 1845, Vol. 14, p. 112. Hereafter quoted as *N.S.A.*

10. Bain, p. 67.

11. ibid., p. 62.

12. *Fasti Ecclesiae Scoticanae*, New edn, Edinburgh, 1926, Vol. 6, p. 476.

13. Sir Aeneas, p. 29.

14. *Old Statistical Account of Scotland*, Edinburgh, 1793, Vol. 8, p. 510. Hereafter quoted as *O.S.A.*

15. The group 'seceded' from the church in 1733. J.H.S. Burleigh, *A Church History of Scotland*, London, 1960, p. 282.

16. ibid., p. 351.

17. Ethel Bassin, *The Old Songs of Skye: Frances Tolmie and her Circle*, London, 1977.

18. Forsyth, pp. 170-7, 282.

19. *N.S.A.*, Vol. 14, p. 107.

20. Forsyth, p. 276.

21. ibid., p. 352.

22. James Robertson, *Journal, 1771*, National Library of Scotland, MS 2508.

3 Over the River

1. Burt, Vol. 2, pp. 55-6.

2. Sir Aeneas, p. 3.

3. Thomas Dick Lauder, *An Account of the Great Floods of August, 1829*, 3rd edn, Elgin, 1873, pp. 28-31.

4. Nock, p. 151.

5. Mitchell, Vol. I, pp. 160-2.

6. Sir Aeneas, pp. 31-2.

7. ibid., p. 32.

8. ibid., p. 32.

9. ibid., p. 33.

10. James Robertson, op. cit.

11. *N.S.A.*, Vol. 14, p. 107.

12. ibid., Vol. 14, p. 103.

13. Sir Aeneas, p. 34.

14. *N.S.A.*, Vol. 14, p. 107.

15. James Robertson, op. cit.

16. *N.S.A.*, Vol. 14, p. 112.

17. ibid., Vol. 14, p. 108.
18. Sir James MacGregor, *Scottish Verse from the Book of the Dean of Lismore*, ed. W.J. Watson, Edinburgh, 1937, pp. 149-51. Hereafter quoted as MacGregor.
19. A.M. Mackintosh, p. 120.

4 The Holding and Use of Land

1. *O.S.A.*, Vol. 8, p. 500.
2. ibid., Vol. 8, p. 501.
3. Forsyth, pp. 160-3.
4. I.F. Grant, *Every-day Life on an Old Highland Farm*, London, 1924, ch. 3, 4, 7. Written by the author and founded upon an account book kept by her great-great-great-grandfather when a tacksman in Badenoch.
5. Estimate based on conclusions for the whole of Scotland in *Scottish Population History from the 17th century to the 1930s*, ed. M.W. Flinn, 1977.
6. James Fraser, *Chronicles of the Frasers: the Wardlaw Manuscript*, Edinburgh, 1905, S.H.S., p. 236. Hereafter quoted as *Wardlaw Manuscript*.
7. Forsyth, pp. 226-7.
8. *Parliamentary Papers*, 1846, XXXVII, pp. 497-507.
9. *O.S.A.*, Vol. 8, p. 507.
10. Sir Aeneas, pp. 30-31.
11. Victor Gaffney, *The Lordship of Strathavon*, Third Spalding Club, Aberdeen, 1960, ch. 1, 2, 3. Victor Gaffney, 'Summer Shealings', *Scottish Historical Review*, Vol. 38, 1959, pp. 20-35.
12. A.M. Mackintosh, pp. 369, 386, 374-5, 389, 484-92, 510-11.
13. ibid., pp. 218, 368-70. A merk was worth one shilling one penny and one third of a penny.
14. John Spalding, *History of the Troubles and Memorable Transactions in Scotland and England from MDCXXIV to MDCXLV.*, Bannatyne Club, Edinburgh, 1828, Vol. 1, pp. 1-2.
15. ibid., pp. 2-6, 9-10.
16. ibid., pp. 9-10. Sir William Fraser, *Chiefs of Clan Grant*, Edinburgh, 1883, Vol. 1, pp. 229-30. Victor Gaffney, *The Lordship of Strathavon*, p. 68.
17. Forsyth, p. 350.
18. A.M. Mackintosh, pp. 213-4.
19. ibid., p. 395.
20. Margaret Mackintosh of Mackintosh, *The Clan Mackintosh and Clan Chattan*, Edinburgh, 1948, pp. 7, 33-5. Hereafter quoted as Mgt Mackintosh.
21. I.F. Grant, *Every-day Life on an Old Highland Farm*, London, 1924, pp. 13-4.
22. C. Fraser-Mackintosh, *Minor Septs of Clan Chattan*, Glasgow, 1898, pp. 10-13, 77. Hereafter quoted as Fraser-Mackintosh.
23. Sir Aeneas, p. 4. The drawing of Moy Hall is reproduced in Mgt Mackintosh, p. 114.
24. William Mackintosh, *An Essay on Ways and Means for Inclosing Fallowing and Planting in Scotland*, Edinburgh, 1729, pp. 229-31.
25. A.M. Mackintosh, pp. 374-5.

26. Fraser-Mackintosh, p. 71.
27. A.M. Mackintosh, *Brigadier Mackintosh of Borlum*, Nairn. Priv. printed, 1918.

5   The Land and the People

1. *O.S.A.*, Vol. 8, p. 502.
2. *N.S.A.*, Vol. 14, p. 106.
3. Fraser-Mackintosh, p. 71.
4. *N.S.A.*, Vol. 14, p. 111.
5. Charles St John, *The Wild Sports and Natural History of the Highlands*, London, 1907, p. 206.
6. Fraser-Mackintosh, pp. 72-3.
7. *N.S.A.*, Vol. 14, p. 110.
8. Hope MacDougall, *The Island of Kerrera*; 2nd edn, Oban, 1979.
9. Seafield Papers, GD 248/1024.
10. *O.S.A.*, Vol. 8, pp. 502, 507, 501.
11. L. Simond, *Journal of a Tour and Residence in Great Britain During the Years 1810 and 1811*, 2nd edn, 2 Vols., Edinburgh, 1817, Vol. 1, p. 395.
12. *N.S.A.*, Vol. 14, p. 107.
13. ibid., p. 108.
14. For a summary of many references see I.F. Grant, *Every-day Life on an Old Highland Farm, 1769-1782*, London, 1924, pp. 99-100, 106. *Parliamentary Papers*, 1846, **XXXVII**, 497-511.
15. Sir Aeneas, p. 28.
16. Fraser-Mackintosh, p. 71.
17. H. Ricketts, *Firearms*, London, 1962, p. 101.
18. Sir Aeneas, p. 15.
19. T. Sinton, *The Poetry of Badenoch*, Inverness, 1906, pp. 500-502.
20. W.G. Stewart, *Lectures on the Mountains; or the Highlands and the Highlanders*, London, 1860.
21. I.F. Grant, 'Some Accounts of Individual Highland Sporting Estates', *Economic Journal* (Econ. Hist. Ser., no. 3), 1928, p. 409.
22. *Departmental Committee on Deer Forests*, 1919, London, 1922, p. 22.
23. I.F. Grant, op. cit., p. 410.
24. *N.S.A.*, Vol. 14, pp. 108. 111.
25. *O.S.A.*, Vol. 8, p. 509.
26. R. Bruce Lockhart, *Scotch*, 4th edn, London, 1970, pp. 10-12.

6   Where All the Roads Meet

1. *N.S.A.*, Vol. 14, p. 99.
2. A.M. Mackintosh, p. 498.
3. Sir Aeneas, p. 36.
4. I.F. Grant, *Social and Economic Development of Scotland before 1603*, Edinburgh, 1930, pp. 308, 543-4. P. Hume Brown, *Early Travellers in Scotland*, Ist edn, 1891, Edinburgh, 1973, p. 87.

5. MacGregor, p. 3.
6. Sir Aeneas, p. 35.
7. Forsyth, p. 352.
8. *Wardlaw Manuscript*, p. xxxvi.

7 Moy and Clan Mackintosh

1. Jean Dunlop, *The Clan Mackintosh*, Edinburgh, 1960, p. 5. A.M. Mackintosh, p. 7.
2. A.M. Mackintosh, p. 217.
3. ibid., pp. 16, 20, 35. Mgt Mackintosh, p. 2.
4. *The Scots Peerage*, Edinburgh, 1904, Vol. 1, pp. 506-7.
5. Sir J. Stewart, *The Camerons*, Stirling, n.d., p. 8.
6. A.M. Mackintosh, pp. 45-66.
7. Sir Aeneas, p. 26.
8. Walter Macfarlane, *Genealogical Collections Concerning Families in Scotland*, Edinburgh, 1900, Scottish History Society, Vol. 1, pp. 185-6.
9. A.M. Mackintosh, pp. 80-81. For subsequent references in this section *see* pp. 103, 132-45, 265-86, 357-8.
10. Sir Aeneas, pp. 61-2. For subsequent references in this section *see* pp. 23-4, 8.
11. Jean Dunlop, op. cit., pp. 15-22.
12. John Lesley, *History of Scotland*, Edinburgh, 1830, Bannatyne Club, p. 137, Jean Dunlop, op. cit., p. 13.
13. Walter Macfarlane, op. cit., Vol. 1, pp. 244-5.
14. *Wardlaw Manuscript*, pp. 453-4.
15. James Philip, *The Grameid*, ed. and tr. A.D. Murdoch, Edinburgh, 1888, Scottish History Society, pp. 54, 127-9.
16. ibid., pp. 179-80.
17. For a summary of the feud *see* A.M. Mackintosh, pp. 285-90.
18. A.M. Mackintosh, pp. 357-8.
19. For a good summary *see* Mgt Mackintosh, pp. 44-5.
20. A.M. Mackintosh, p. 320. For subsequent references in this section *see* pp. 294, 298-310, 395, 515.
21. Sir Aeneas, p. 28. For subsequent references in this section *see* pp. 20, 25, 27, 29-32.
22. Mgt Mackintosh, pp. 38.
23. A.M. Mackintosh in his *The Mackintoshes and Clan Chattan* has a footnote on p. 331 stating that Mackintosh was appointed a Captain in the Black Watch. For the sake of the narrative it is important to stress that he was actually in Lord Loudon's army as stated in Lord Elcho's *A Short Account of the Affairs in Scotland in the Years 1744, 1745 and 1746*, p. 390. Also in Forbes's *The Lyon in Mourning*, Edinburgh, Scottish History Society, Vol. I, p. 150.
24. A.M. Mackintosh, p. 331. For subsequent references in this section *see* pp. 331, 336, 340-354.
25. Cope embarked his troops at Aberdeen, disembarking them at Dunbar and was defeated at Prestonpans.
26. R. McGillivray, 'The Officers of the Mackintosh Regiment, 1746', *Clan Chattan Journal*, 1980, Vol. 7 (4), pp. 198-209.

27. Forbes, op. cit., Vol. I, p. 150.

28. Allan Maclean, 'Stairsneach nan Gaidheal and the Rout of Moy', *Clan Chattan Journal*, 1979, Vol. 7 (3), pp. 130-32.

29. R. McGillivray, op. cit., p. 199 gives this revised estimate of the Mackintosh losses.

30. For a general outline of the battle *see* D. Daiches, *Prince Charles Edward Stuart*, London, 1973, pp. 206-18.

31. James Stuart, *March of the Highland Army in the Years 1745-1746*, Miscellany of the Spalding Club, Aberdeen, 1841, Vol. 1, p. 343.

32. Letter in the Seafield Papers.

33. I am indebted to Mr George Dixon for this information.

34. Frank Adam, *The Clans, Septs and Regiments of the Scottish Highlands*, 8th edn rev., Edinburgh, 1975, p. 371.

35. A.M. Mackintosh, pp. 354-5.

36. Sir Aeneas, p. 56. For subsequent references *see* pp. 12, 16-17, 44, 54, 57.

37. Mgt Mackintosh, pp. 58-9.

8 Traffic on the Two Roads

1. Haldane, op. cit., p. 11.

2. Mitchell, Vol. I, p. 318.

3. Frank Adam, op. cit., p. 440.

4. R.M. Barnes, *The Uniforms and History of the Scottish Regiments*, London, 1956, p. 64.

5. ibid., Appendix I.

6. Mitchell, Vol. I, p. 318.

Select Index